MW01634210

Live Yoga

Live Yoga

The Yoga Sutras
of Patanjali
for Modern Times

Anand Krishna

Penerbit PT Gramedia Pustaka Utama, Jakarta

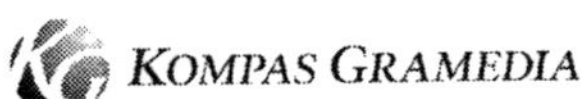

Contents

"You can enter yoga, or the path of yoga,
only when you are totally frustrated
with your own mind as it is.
If you are still hoping that you can gain
something through your mind,
yoga is not for you.

Osho (1931-1990)

Mystic, Philosopher & Spiritual Mentor

Samādhi Pādaḥ
Enlightenment: The Purpose

Sādhanā Pādaḥ
Practice: Soul Work-In

Vibhuti Pādaḥ
Glory: Do not Stop, Go Beyond!

Kaivalya Pādaḥ
Suchness/Oneness: The Ultimate

Yoga: The Universal Sindhu
Spiritual Values for One and All
≈ a word before we part ≈

*"True yoga is control of the senses.
One should treat alike both praise
and censure, pleasure and pain.
This kind of self-restraint is yoga."*

Sathya Sai Baba (1926-2011)
Mystic, Social Reformer & Spiritual Mentor

SINDHU, SHINTU, HINDU, INDIES, INDIA, HINDIA & YOGA

≈ a preface ≈

*"Those who cannot remember the past
are condemned to repeat it."*

George Santayana (1863-1952)
Pilosopher, Essayist, Poet and Novelist

"Those who cannot learn from history are doomed to repeat it; Those who do not remember their past are condemned to repeat their mistakes; Those who do not read history are doomed to repeat it; Those who fail to learn from the mistakes of their predecessors are destined to repeat them; Those who do not know history's mistakes are doomed to repeat them." We have heard phrases like these a thousand times, yet we keep forgetting. So, we are condemned to repeat the same lessons over and over.

Empires, entire nations and civilizations have fallen from grace, disintegrated, fragmented and turned to dust because of this very reason. Many of them are totally forgotten, as if they never existed. Indeed, those who do not remember history are forgotten by history.

We may have also read the following reminder by Edmund Burke (1729-1797), an Irish Statesman of yesteryears:

"People will not look forward to posterity, who never look backward to their ancestors."

Alas, all such reminders have fallen on deaf ears. Even now, we can find communities, even nations at the brink of disintegration for the very same reason. We must learn from them so as not to make the same mistakes.

Decades ago, Nobel laureate V.S. Naipaul warned us of what could happen in countries, where a foreign culture is forcibly imposed upon an indigenous one. And, he particularly mentioned countries belonging to the great civilization of Sindhu Valley.

The first most clear traces and remnants of this great civilization were found in a region, now part of the modern Islamic Republic of Pakistan. The ruins of Mohen-jo-daro, recognized as the cradle of this ancient civilization stand witness to its greatness.

It was the great Arab historian of the 10th century BC, Al Beruni, who mispronounced Sindhu as Hindu. The historian collectively called all the lands and the islands beyond the Sindh valley (now part of the Islamic Republic of Pakistan) "Hind".

He was not the first to mispronounce the word. Much earlier, the Chinese had called it Shintu or Shin-tuh. There are indications that the early Arabs knew about Sindhu civilization from the Chinese merchants and some of the tribes abbreviated it to Shin.

A thousand years later, Al Beruni's magnum opus on the Indian Civilization is still in print and remains an interesting read. The great historian wrote about the civilization with an unparalleled passion, translated various spiritual and other texts into Arabic and glorified the people as worshipers of "One" God, as can be clearly seen in the following passage taken from the above mentioned book:

> *"With regard to God, the Hindus believe that he is one, eternal, without beginning and end, acting by free will, almighty, all-wise, living, giving life, ruling, and preserving; one who is unique in his sovereignty, beyond all likeness and unlikeness, and neither resembling anything nor having anything resemble him.*

> *"In order to illustrate this, we shall produce some extracts from the Hindu literature, lest the reader should think that our account is nothing but hearsay.*

> *"In the book of Patanjali (the author is, perhaps, referring to a treatise based on the Yoga Sutras of Patanjali – a.k.) the pupil asks: 'Who is the worshipped one, by the worship of whom blessing is obtained?'*

"The master says: 'It is he who, being eternal and unique, does not for his part stand in need of any human action for which he might give as a recompense either a blissful repose, which is hoped and longed for, or a troubled existence, which is feared and dreaded. He is unattainable to thought, being sublime beyond all unlikeness which is abhorrent and all likeness which is sympathetic. By his essence he knows from all eternity. Knowledge, in the human sense of the term, has as its object that which was unknown before, whilst not knowing does not apply to God at any time or in any condition."

This was of course not acceptable to Sultan Mahmud, the ruler of Ghazna, who wanted religious justification for the looting of the Indian Subcontinent. The book, therefore, was published after Mahmud's death.

Much later, when the Moguls came to India and settled there, they called their kingdom

Hindustan. "Hindu" was never used to identify a certain religion, but rather a civilization as well as the geographical location. The Portuguese did the same when they distorted the word further into "Indies". Later, the British pronounced it India.

Interestingly, even one of the great Indonesian freedom fighters, Cokroaminoto, the founder of Syarikat Islam, called his newspaper *Utusan Hindia*, literally meaning the "*Hindian* Messenger", implying that *Hindia* did not refer to a particular religion, but to a cultural and geographical region.

Nusantarans of old and modern Indonesians shared this very same civilization with the ancient Iranians, the Afghans and the peoples of Bharat (present day Indian subcontinent).

As pointed out by Coedes, the French historian, the mainland Indian rulers never colonized the subcontinent. They did not have to impose their spiritual and cultural values since the entire region shared with them those values.

The westerners called the Indonesian archipelago ancient Nusantara or Dvipantara, lesser India, a misnomer though it recognized the fact that the peoples of the entire region belonged to the same civilization.

The Nusantarans were not "lesser" in any way. Indeed, the Indonesian archipelago was recognized as Svarna Dvipa, the gold-yielding islands. The seas creating geographical separation did not separate the peoples culturally. They shared the same cultural roots.

Yoga as a science developed from such roots. So, we find Yoga in its various forms all over the Indian subcontinent and on the islands of Indonesia. Yoga has nothing to do with any *"ism"*, any religious creed, dogma, or doctrine, but with "Hindu" as a civilization.

"Hinduism" as religion is a fact that must be recognized today, so are the ancient indigenous belief systems of the Sundanese, the Javanese, and others living on the Indonesian archipelago. All these belief systems are as much a part of the Great Sindhu, Shintu or Hindu civilization as Yoga is. That, however, does not reduce Yoga into a religion or a sectarian belief system, as the words religion and belief are being defined today.

Any ardent student of cultural history of the region can easily discover that the word Yoga was already in use thousands of years before the word "Hindu" came into common usage. If we are to use Al Beruni's terms, then the peoples of the modern Indian and Pakistani Republics, a major part of Indo-China and the Indonesian Archipelago are all Hindus. It is not surprising therefore, if the Indian pilgrims performing haj in Arabia were called Hindi Hajis until sometime ago.

Our common ancestors, the Hindus of old, belonging to the Sindhu valley civilization, developed Yoga as a comprehensive and holistic system for general wellbeing. They did not create any dogma or doctrine around it. They did not reduce it to some sectarian teaching.

That Yoga has its roots in the Hindu cultural values and Hindu civilization is a historical fact that cannot be denied. It remains, however, free from any *ism*, as, indeed the universal Hindu spiritual values are.

To connect Yoga with any *ism* would be like connecting Newton's law of gravity with Christianity because Newton who discovered it was Christian or the theory of relativity with Judaism because Albert Einstein had Jewish blood running through his veins.

What about the numeral "O" then? Or, the science of astronomy? The Arabs first learnt it from the peoples of Sindh and later brought them to the west. Is it safe to use the same? It is indeed a shame that some groups of people reject Yoga without even understanding what Yoga is about. But, then, it is their own loss.

On the other hand, there are people who have reduced Yoga to a commodity. These are people thriving on the commercialization of Yoga.

Yoga is a life style; it is not merely a set of exercises or dry philosophy that can be mastered by taking a 100, 200, 500, 1000, or 10,000 hours program and becoming a certified teacher.

One must live Yoga, must practice it, and must transform one's entire life before sharing it. Yes, sharing it. For, a true practitioner of Yoga or a true Yogi shall never ever claim to be a teacher. A Yogi, at the most, is a facilitator and nothing more. A true Yogi practices before preaching.

Alas, the world today is abound with pseudo Yogis exhibiting their certificates for monetary gain alone. There are many who have no inkling of what Yoga is, and, yet, they are called Yoga teachers and instructors.

———❈———

For any true practitioner of Yoga, the study of the *Yoga Sutras of Patanjali* is not only imperative, but also part of his/her *sadhana* or Yoga practice.

At the time of his call for the adoption of June 21st as the International Yoga Day, the Indian Prime Minister Narendra Modi rightly pointed out before the UN General Assembly (September 27, 2014) that:

> *"Yoga is an invaluable gift of India's ancient tradition.*
>
> *It embodies unity of mind and body; thought and action;*
>
> *restraint and fulfilment; harmony between man and nature;*
>
> *a holistic approach to health and well-being.*
>
> *It is not about exercise but to discover the sense of oneness with yourself, the world and the nature."*

An unprecedented 177 of the total 193 member states of the UN co-sponsored the resolution on the International Yoga Day. At the same time, one wonders if the explanation of Yoga given by the Indian Prime Minister Narendra Modi has been properly understood.

For many self-styled Yoga-entrepreneurs and Yoga-certification industry, the adoption of June 21 as International Yoga Day is nothing but an additional tool for marketing Yoga as commodity. For them, Yoga is but a set of gym-like exercises, that is all. Indeed, there are entrepreneurs who scoff at the idea of Yoga beyond what is convenient to sell.

Sometime back, Al-Jazeera aired two shows on Yoga. The comments made by the prominent, some very big names, that Yoga is "this" and also "that" are very surprising and disturbing. They are equally guilty for the present, unfortunate state of Yoga, as it is turning into a commodity. There can be no two, no different definitions of medicine or economics or mathematics. The basic definition of each of those and other disciplines is one and the same. It is the same with Yoga.

Yoga is a holistic philosophy, covering all aspects of life. The purpose being enlightenment, *samadhi*, often translated as equilibrium or equanimity. It is a state of being, and a quality to live. And, if one goes a step further, then it is through Yoga practice that one realises oneness, in Sanskrit *kaivalya*, the literal translation of which would be "suchness".

This is a state of being, where one realises the oneness of all creation, all existence, and where one realises the interconnection and interdependency of all living beings, all living organism. Thus, one can no longer remain indifferent toward the suffering of not only fellow human beings, but fellow living beings.

———∞———

A Yogi, that is a true practitioner of Yoga, cannot be violent. A Yogi cannot be intolerant. He/she is not a power-monger. There are certain end-results expected of a Yogi from practicing Yoga as life discipline.

Unfortunately, many of those engaged in "selling" Yoga are not familiar with those values. They are not even familiar with the basic texts such as the *Yoga Sutras* of Patanjali (the prime most text), *Bhagavad Gita*, and *Hatha Yoga* Pradipika.

They are more concerned with certifications, alliances, and et cetera, with monetary gain as their main aim and sole purpose. To discard all these texts and given to egoistic notion that one can learn Yoga without referring to them betrays one's ignorance and vanity.

Our heads may spin upon researching the background of most of the "certification agencies". One wonders if Krishna, Buddha or Patanjali, the great masters of Yoga, had any certification. Forget the oldies and the divines, even Shivananda, or, more recent Iyengar had no certification.

Unfortunately however, even those associated with such sane names are now given to insanity, to this mad rush to make money by selling Yoga.

Yoga, once again, is a way of life. One who does not live Yoga can never ever share the Yogi way of life.

Certificates issued by them are worthless. The real Yogis are *Acharyas*, they teach by their own life example. One, two, or five hundred hours of training cannot turn you into a Yogi. It is a lifetime *sadhana* or spiritual practice. *Wake up and be a True Yogi!*

This new, fresh translation of the sutras of Patanjali is being offered to you, to awaken the Spirit of True Yogi within you, within each one of us.

yoga ve jayati bhuri ayoga bhurisankhayo
etam dvedhapatham natva bhavaya vibhavaya
ca tatha ttanam niveseyya
yatha bhuri pavaddhati.

Indeed, wisdom is born of Yoga;
without Yoga, wisdom is lost.
Knowing this twofold path of gain
and loss of wisdom,
one should conduct oneself so that
wisdom may increase.

Buddha
Dhammapada, Verse 282

THE YOGA SUTRAS OF PATANJALI

≈ a transcreation ≈

Samādhi Pādaḥ
Enlightenment: The Purpose

I.1

atha yoga-anuśāsanam

*Thus, discipline or life governed
by certain values is Yoga.*

I.2

yogaś-citta-vṛtti-nirodhaḥ

*Yoga is the cessation of the vṛttis or modifications
of citta or mind at its very core,
i.e. the seeds of thoughts and emotions.*

I.3

tadā draṣṭuḥ svarūpe-'vasthānam

*Then (when the cessation of citta vṛttis,
the modifications of mind at its core level
is achieved), the Jivātmā or individual soul
is at its original state as the witness.*

I.4

vṛtti sārūpyam-itaratra

*Otherwise (when the citta or the mind
is not yet restrained at its core),
the Jivātmā or individual soul identifies
itself with all the modifications happening
to the citta, the mind-core, or the mind-seed.*

I.5

vṛttayaḥ pañcatayyaḥ kliṣṭākliṣṭāḥ

*There are five different types of citta vṛttis,
or modifications at the mind-seed
or mind-core level
either causing affliction or not.*

I.6

pramāṇa viparyaya vikalpa nidrā smṛtayaḥ

*Pramāṇa or right cognition or knowledge;
Viparyaya or false knowledge;
Vikalpa or imagination; Nidrā or sleep;
and Smṛti or memory –*

*these are the five vṛttis or modifications
either causing afflictions or not.*

I.7

pratyakṣa-anumāna-āgamāḥ
pramāṇāni

*Pramāṇa, right cognition or knowledge
has three sources:
Pratyakṣa or direct experience;
Anumāna or assumption;
and Āgamaḥ or words of the wise
that can be trusted.*

I.8

viparyayo mithyā-jñānam-atadrūpa
pratiṣṭham

*Viparyaya or false knowledge has
no base in reality.*

I.9

śabda-jñāna-anupātī vastu-śūnyo vikalpaḥ

*Knowledge and words without any substance
are called Vikalpa or imagination.*

I.10

abhāva-pratyaya-ālambanā tamo-vṛttir-nidra

*Modifications (or changes at
the mind core level experienced) during sleep
or Nidra have no substance as well.*

I.11

anu-bhūta-viṣaya-asaṁpramoṣaḥ smṛtiḥ

*Smṛti or memory causes the individual soul
or Jivātmā unable to disconnect
or detach itself from the past experiences.*

I.12

abhyāsa-vairāgya-ābhyāṁ tan-nirodhaḥ

Nirodha *or cessation of all such*
modifications of citta
or the mind core is possible by means
of abhyāsa, *repetitive and intensive effort;*
and vairāgya *or detachment.*

I.13

tatra sthitau yatno'bhyāsaḥ

Abhyāsa *or intensive*
and repetitive effort, indeed,
is hard, hence, must be practised
whole-heartedly
(and with a strong determination).

I.14

sa tu dīrghakāla nairantarya satkāra-ādara-āsevito dṛḍhabhūmiḥ

With consistent, intensive and repetitive effort
in full devotion, i.e. in full awareness

and without a feeling of being burdened,
one becomes grounded in one's practice
(in restraining or stopping the modifications
of citta or the mind core – this is abhyāsa).

I.15

dṛṣṭa-anuśravika-viṣaya-vitṛṣṇasya vaśīkāra-saṁjñā vairāgyam

Vairāgya *or perfect detachment is attained,*
when one is neither disturbed nor
tempted by the viṣaya,
sense objects and conditions outside,
neither by what one sees, nor by what one hears
about. Thus, one attains to the state of
Saṁjñā *or perfect, true knowingness*
(free of all conflicts arising from a sense
of duality).

I.16

tatparaṁ puruṣa-khyāteḥ guṇa-vaitṛṣṇyam

(The perfect or true knowingness is about)
Puruṣa *or the collective individual soul*
that is not affected by guṇas

*or the qualities of matter
and material existence; not attached to it,
and does not crave for it
(this, indeed, is also the true detachment
or vairāgya).*

I.17

vitarka-vicāra-ānanda-asmitā-rupa-anugamāt-samprajñātaḥ

Samprajñātah is a state of Samādhi
*or enlightenment
that is accompanied by the perfect knowingness
about one's true identity;
yet, not fully free from the sense of duality.
It is based on* Vitarka *or reasoning;*
Vicāra, *deliberation or reflection;*
Ānanda *or bliss that arises
from one's own being;
and,* Asmitā, *I-ness, or self realization
(as* Jivā *or individual soul that is part of*
Puruṣa *or collective soul, that, in turn, is never
separated from* Paramātmā *or
the Supreme Soul).*

I.18

virāma-pratyaya-abhyāsa-pūrvaḥ
samskāra-śeṣo-'nyaḥ

The State (of Asamprajñāta) is Samādhi
or enlightenment that is accompanied by
the perfect knowingness about
one's true identity and, free from any sense of
duality. Yet, it carries pūrva samskāra
or impressions from the past, which can be
overcome or eliminated by consistent, i.e.
repetitive and intensive effort with
a determintation to overcome them.

I.19

bhava-pratyayo videha-prakṛti-
layānam

Having attained to the state of videha
or having dropped the physical body
(and the elements, which the physical body is made
of have already joined their respective principles in
the nature or prakṛti), a strong will to
"become" again
(or to experience rebirth) may still survive.

I.20

śraddhā-vīrya-smṛti samādhi-prajñā-pūrvaka itareṣām

*Some of them (thus reborn) may attain
to the state of* Samādhi *or enlightenment,
by the merit of prajñā* pūrvakaḥ *or past efforts,
added with (present efforts undertaken with)*
śraddhā *or full faith;*
vīrya *or courage; and* smṛti *or attentiveness.*

I.21

tīvra-saṁvegānām-āsannaḥ

*Those who speed up (work hard for it)
reach their goal (of* Samādhi,
equanimity or enlightenment) faster.

I.22

mṛdu-madhya-adhimātratvāt-tato'pi viśeṣaḥ

*The difference (the time it takes to
reach the goal) depends upon one's speed
(intensity); it may be slow, medium, or fast.*

I.23

īśvara-praṇidhānād-vā

*Or (meaning, Samādhi or enlightenment
can also be attained by means of)
Īśvara Praṇidhāna, total submission
to the Lord
who dwells within all beings
and envelopes all as well
(One who is both transcendent and imminent).*

I.24

kleśa karma vipāka-āśayaiḥ-aparāmṛṣṭaḥ puruṣa-viśeṣa īśvaraḥ

*Īśvara is Puruṣa or collective soul
(consisting of innumerable individual souls,
as sunlight comprises of uncountable sunrays)
that is not affected by inflictions; activities
(be they physical, mental, or emotional);
the consequence of any activity; and
the impressions of activities done in the past*

I.25

tatra niratiśayaṁ sarvajña-bījam

*There (in the Lord, the Supreme
Being or Paramātmā,
the Singular Cause of Puruṣa, Energy or Soul;
and Prakṛti, Matter or Material Existence)
lay the seed of omniscience that is unsurpassed.*

I.26

sa eṣa pūrveṣām-api-guruḥ
kālena-anavacchedāt

*Being infinite or unlimited by time,
That (the Lord, Paramātmā, the Supreme One, the
Cause of Energy and Matter or Puruṣa and Prakṛti)
is the (True) Guru, the True Master of every one
from the most ancient ones.*

I.27

tasya vācakaḥ praṇavaḥ

*The verbal expression of That
(the Lord, Paramātmā, or the Supreme One)
is the Praṇava, the primeval sound of Om.*

I.28

taj-japaḥ tad-artha-bhāvanam

*By repeating It (Om or Aum) constantly,
one realises Its very meaning or purpose.*

I.29

tataḥ pratyak-cetana-adhigamo-
‘py-antarāya-abhavaś-ca

*Thus, Pratyak Cetana or inner/soul-consciousness
is attained, and all obstacles removed or
overcome.*

I.30

vyādhi styāna saṁśaya
pramāda-ālasya-avirati
bhrāntidarśana-alabdha-
bhūmikatva-
anavasthitatvāni citta-vikṣepāḥ te
antarāyāḥ

*Obstacles distorting the mind core or citta are
Vyādhi or disease; Styāna or dullness;
Saṁśaya or doubt;*

Pramāda, *carelessness and/
or negligance arising from ego;*
Alasya *or laziness;*
Avirati *or indulgence in sensory pleasures;*
Bhrāntidarśana, *conditioned/false view, confusion,
or delusion;*
Alabdha-Bhūmikatva *not grounded, or not realistic;*
and Anavasthitatvāni *or instability.*

I.31

duḥkha-daurmanasya-aṅgamejayatva-śvāsapraśvāsāḥ vikṣepa sahabhuvaḥ

*Such mental distractions are all followed by
Dukha, suffering, sorrow, or a feeling of emptyness;
Daurmanasya, depression or nervousness;
Aṅgam and* Śvāsa-Praśvāsāḥ *Ejatva or
unsteadiness of limbs and irregular breathing.*

I.32

tat-pratiṣedha-artham-eka-tattva-abhyāsaḥ

*To counteract and remove (such obstacles,
mental inflictions and distractions),
the only way is abhyāsa, constant, intensive
and repetitive practice (of the following):*

I.33

maitrī karuṇā mudito-pekṣāṇāṁ-sukha-duḥkha puṇya-apuṇya-viṣayāṇāṁ bhāvanātaḥ citta-prasādanam

*Maitrī, friendliness; Karunā, compassion;
Muditā, joyfulness; and Upekṣā or equanimity,
that is being indifferent towards all dualistic
experiences, such as sukha and dukha
or pleasure and pain and the like.
Thus the citta or mind core is clarified
or so cleansed that it is no longer distracted
by the triggers without and within.*

I.34

pracchardana-vidhāraṇa-ābhyāṁ vā prāṇasya

*Or, by expulsion (exhalation) and retention
or holding of Prāṇa, the life force
(by regulating one's breathing).*

I.35

viṣayavatī vā pravṛtti-rutpannā manasaḥ sthiti nibandhinī

*Maṇah or mind can also be steadied by
being attentive to the sensory perception
(arising from the contact of senses with the
sense objects, certain conditions or triggers).*

I.36

viśokā vā jyotiṣmatī

*Or, (by meditating on) the inner light
(thus going) beyond all inflictions and sorrows.*

I.37

vītarāga viṣayam vā cittam

Or, by fixing the citta, *mind-core,*
or mind-seed on
those who are free of attachment
toward the (sense) objects.

I.38

svapna-nidrā jñāna-ālambanam vā

Or, by holding on to jñāna *or true knowledge*
obtained from (intuitive) dream
and/or (deep, meditative) sleep.

I.39

yathā-abhimata-dhyānād-vā

Or, by meditating upon or by being attentive to
what you desire for (and truly believe in).

I.40

paramāṇu parama-mahattva-anto-'sya vaśīkāraḥ

(Thus by restraining citta *or the mind core
through meditation or being attentive)
anything from the smallest part of atom to
the vast infinite existence can be brought under
control.*

I.41

kṣīṇa-vṛtter-abhijātasy-eva maṇer-grahītṛ-grahaṇa-grāhyeṣu tatstha-tadañjanatā samāpattiḥ

The state of the citta, *the mind core;
and, the* manaḥ, *the mind
that is no longer affected by* vṛttis, *modifications,
changes, disturbances, and distractions – can be
likened to that of a transparant gem or clear crystal.
It is not disturbed by the changes
experienced by the experiencer,
the act of experiencing, and what is experienced.
Having attained to this state called*
Samāpattiḥ *or unity*

of the experiencer, the experience,
and the experienced,
it simply reflects things as they are.

I.42

tatra śabdārtha-jñāna-vikalpaiḥ saṁkīrṇā savitarkā samāpattiḥ

(There are different levels of state
of Samāpattiḥ or unity.
The first one being) Savitarkā Samāpattiḥ,
wherein Jñāna *or true knowingness is still disturbed*
by words and their meanings,
or the very purpose of those words.
(This confusion is overcome by tarka *or intelligent*
reasoning.)

I.43

smṛti-pariśuddhau svarūpa-śūnyeva-arthamātra-nirbhāsā nirvitarkā

(The second level of unity or Samāpattiḥ
is referred to as) Nirvitarkā Samāpattiḥ,
when tarka *or intelligent reasoning*

is trancended (for, it is no longer needed).
Thus, the mind cleansed of even memories of
all past impressions is as good as śūnya, non-
existing, devoid of its very form as mind.
In such a state, then, the end-purpose
of having the mind alone remains, i.e.
enlightenment or Samādhi.

I.44

etayaiva savicārā nirvicārā ca sūkṣma-viṣaya vyākhyātā

Similarly (the third and fourth levels
of the state of unity or Samāpattiḥ)
are referred to as Savicāra, with subtle
memory or reflection;
and Nirvicāra, *without even subtle memory*
or reflection of past events and conditions.

I.45

sūkṣma-viṣayatvam-ca-aliṅga paryavasānam

Indeed, such subtle memory of
past events and conditions,

*although alinga or unmanifest, must also
be overcome and brought to an end.*

I.46

tā eva sabījas-samādhiḥ

*Such is referred to as sabījaḥ samādhi.
(Meaning, not entirely condition-free
state of enlightenment. For, it still carries
memory-seeds or bījaḥ that
can sprout anytime giving rise to other subtle or
gross conditions, and affecting one's meditation
or meditative state.)*

I.47

nirvicāra-vaiśāradye-'dhyātma-prasādaḥ

*By attaining and skilfully maintaining
Nirvicāra Samāpattiḥ
or the condition-free state of unity,
the true (spiritual) soul-conciousness arises.*

I.48

ṛtaṁbharā tatra prajñā

(In the state of Nirvicāra Samāpattiḥ)
one's Prajñā, *wisdom, intelligence,*
or higher knowingness is filled
with ṛtaṁ *or righteousness;*
in other words, having attained to such state,
one's actions become righteous.

I.49

śruta-anumāna-prajñā-abhyām-
anya-viṣayā viśeṣa-arthatvāt

Such state of Prajñā *or higher and deeper*
knowingness is based upon one's direct
and personal experience
(leading to self-realization and righteous action). It
differs from the knowledge gained from others,
or through some assumptions.

I.50

tajjas-saṁskāro-'nya-saṁskāra pratibandhī

Indeed, saṁskāraḥ *or impressions
arising from this state (of* Prajñā *or true
knowingness)
hinders all other impressions.
(Thus, leading one to attain perfection
in* Samādhi, *or the perfect enlightenment.)*

I.51

*tasyāpi nirodhe sarva-nirodhān-
nirbījaḥ samādhiḥ*

Having eliminated all such saṁskāraḥ *or
impressions, all (other hurdles) are eliminated;
and one attains the state of* Nirbijaḥ Samādhi,
the seedless, conditionless perfect enlightenment.

Sādhanā Pādaḥ

Practice: Soul Work-In

II.1

tapaḥ svādhyāy-eśvarapraṇidhānāni kriyā-yogaḥ

Tapaḥ, austerity or self-discipline;
Svādhyāya, *self-study*
of the scriptures, or study of the self –
one's true nature; and, Iśvara Prāṇidhāna,
submission, surrender,
or dedication to Iśvara,
the Lord illuminating one's own being –
these are Kriyā Yoga,
the Yoga *or disciplines of action.*
(In other words, Yoga *is an applicable science.)*

II.2

samādhi-bhāvana-arthaḥ kleśa tanū-karaṇa-arthaś-ca

*These (*Kriyās *or disciplined actions)*
are meant for cultivating or manifesting Samādhi
Bhāvana,
the state of equanimity, or enlightenment;
and (gradually) diminish all kleśas *or afflictions.*

II.3

avidyā-asmitā-rāga-dveṣa-abhiniveśaḥ kleśāḥ

Avidyā *or ignorance;* Asmitā *or I-ness;*
Rāga, *attraction or like;*
Dveṣa, *aversion or dislike;*
and Abhiniveśa *or desire to hold an*
a certain state,
condition, or experience, including
the desire to hold on to life itself,-
these are the causes of kleśa *or affliction.*

II.4

avidyā kṣetram-uttareṣām prasupta-tanu-vicchinn-odārāṇām

Avidyā *or ignorance is the ground,*
the root cause of all other
causes of kleśa *or affliction*
(i.e. asmitā *or i-ness;* rāga-dveṣa *or*
attraction and aversion, like and dislike,
and abhiniveśa *or desire to*
hold on or to cling on
something or some experience),
no matter such kleśa *or infliction are dormant,*

diminished or diminishing;
in other words, they are suppressed,
momentary interrupted, but waiting to
reappear anytime or still fully active.

II.5

anityā-aśuci-duḥkha-anātmasu nitya-śuci-sukha-ātmakhyātir-avidyā

Avidyā *or ignorance causes one*
to mistake or misperceive
the impermanent as permanent,
the impure as pure, the painful as pleasant and
the non-self or non-reality as self or reality.

II.6

dṛg-darśana-śaktyor-ekātmata-iva-asmitā

Asmitā *or i-ness is a state when*
the proweses, the energies of
dṛg *or "the act of seeing"*
and the darśana *or "what is seen"*
appear as one.

II.7

sukha-anuśayī rāgaḥ

Rāga or attraction is the act of clinging to sukha,
or what is perceived as pleasant.

II.8

duḥkha-anuśayī dveṣaḥ

Dveṣa or aversion is the act of
clinging to duḥkha
or what is perceived as unpleasant.

II.9

svarasvāhi viduṣo'pi
samārūḍho'bhiniveśaḥ

Sustained by svarasa or one's own essence,
one's own inner feeling –
even the wise can be dominated,
can be overpowered by abhiniveśa,
the desire for continuity,
the desire to cling to some experience,
something, or someone –
including the desire to go on living.

II.10

te pratiprasava-heyāḥ sūkṣmāḥ

The subtle kleśa *or affliction
(meaning, those not fully manifest)
can be overcome or avoided
by tracing them back to their origin.*

II.11

dhyāna heyāḥ tad-vṛttayaḥ

*The fluctuations, modifications,
disturbances or* vṛttis *arising from
such afflictions or* kleśa *can be avoided
or overcome by* dhyāna *or meditation.*

II.12

kleśa-mūlaḥ karma-aśayo
dṛṣṭa-adṛṣṭa-janma-vedanīyaḥ

Rooted in kleśa *or affliction,
the reservoir (the accumulation)
of* karmas *or actions is the cause
of seen as well as unseen existence
(the present as well as future life-times).*

II.13

sati mūle tad-vipāko jāty-āyur-bhogāḥ

As long as the root cause of karmas exists –
meaning as long as kleśas or afflictions exist –
the fruitition of karmas is certain, undoubtable;
resulting in birth, life-span and various life
experiences.

II.14

te hlāda paritāpa-phalāḥ puṇya-apuṇya-hetutvāt

The fruits or concequences of such actions
or karmas
(rooted in kleśa or afflictions)
can be partaken joyously or sorrowfully,
meaning they can have joyous
or sorrowful impact following the cause
of such actions, whether meritorious,
noble or demeritorious, not noble.

II.15

pariṇāma tāpa saṁskāra duḥkhaiḥ guṇa-vṛtti-virodhācca duḥkham-eva sarvaṁ vivekinaḥ

Those who have developed viveka, *the ability or power to discern, to discriminate (between the true bliss that comes from self-realization and the sensory pleasure derived from body, senses and mind composite), realize that even the* saṁskāra *or impressions of past experiences and actions result in nothing but* tāpa *or anxiety and* duḥkha *or suffering. Similarly,* vṛtti *or fluctuations of mind and conflicting* guṇas *or inherent qualities of all matter cause nothing but pain and suffering.*

II.16

heyaṁ duḥkham-anāgatam

The suffering yet to come in the future can and must be avoided.

II.17

draṣṭṛ-dṛśyayoḥ saṁyogo heyahetuḥ

*The cause (of the suffering) that can,
and is to be avoided is the confusion
arising from* saṁyoga *or the meeting and
correlation between the* dṛśya
or the seen and the draṣṭṛ *or the seer.*

II.18

prakāśa-kriyā-sthiti-śīlaṁ bhūtendriya-ātmakaṁ bhoga-apavarga-arthaṁ dṛśyam

Dṛśyam *or the seen, consisting of
the* bhūta *or elements (i.e. earth, water, fire,
air and the etheric substance of the space) and*
indriya *or senses has (the threefold) nature or* śīla
of prakāśa *or light, thus enligthening (*sattva*),* kriyā
*or dynamism (*rajas*) and* sthiti *or static (*tamas*).
Its very purpose being to provide oneself (*ātmaka*)
with* bhoga *or various enjoyments,
as well as* apavarga *or turning away
from such enjoyments, i.e. liberation.*

II.19

viśeṣa-aviśeṣa-liṅga-mātra-aliṅgāni guṇaparvāṇi

*These are the four states or conditions of
the guṇas or qualities (as mentioned in the
previous sutra): Viśeṣa, distinct or special;
Aviśeṣa, indistinct or common
Liṅga, marked, designated, or manifest; and
Aliṅgāni, unmarked, not-designated, or unmanifest.*

II.20

draṣṭā dṛśimātraḥ śuddho'pi pratyaya-anupaśyaḥ

*Although appearing as seeing or looking, the seer
or Draṣṭā is actually ever pure, ever unaffected.*

II.21

tadartha eva dṛśyasya-ātmā

*The seen (material existence) exists
for the sake of the seer, the eternal witness
(the true self or soul, both as Jivātmā
or individual soul and Puruṣa or collective soul).*

II.22

kṛtārthaṁ pratinaṣṭam-apy-anaṣṭaṁ tadanya sādhāraṇatvāt

It (the existence or prakṛti) *disappears
and becomes non-existent
to those (individual souls or* Jivātmā),
*whose purpose is served and fulfilled.
But, it remains active and existent to those
whose purpose is not fully served or not fulfilled yet.*

II.23

svasvāmi-śaktyoḥ svarūp-oplabdhi-hetuḥ saṁyogaḥ

Saṁyoga, *coming together or union of
two* śaktis *or forces of sva or self
(indicating lower or material self, i.e.
body-mind composite self
produced by* prakṛti *or material existence)
and* Svāmī, *the master of self
(indicating the higher or true self
manifesting as* Puruṣa *or collective soul
and* Jivātmā *or individual soul)
is for the purpose of gaining knowledge
about its* svarūpa, *true form or true nature.*

II.24

tasya hetur-avidyā

*Avidyā or ignorance is the cause
(of such union as mentioned in the
earlier sutra, thus creating duality
as well as the desire to gain knowledge).*

II.25

tad-abhābāt-saṁyoga-abhāvo hānaṁ taddṛśeḥ kaivalyam

*With avidyā or ignorance dispelled,
saṁyoga or the union (of Prakṛti
or material existence and soul or Puruṣa) is
terminated, thus liberation from the seen is attained.*

II.26

viveka-khyātir-aviplavā hānopāyaḥ

*By the constant and conscious practise
or use of viveka, that is the faculty of discernment
or discrimination, one can escape or overcome
avidyā or ignorance.*

II.27

tasya saptadhā prānta-bhūmiḥ prajña

Prajñā *or the state of highest wisdom is attained through seven consecutive stages:*

II.28

yoga-aṅga-anuṣṭhānād-aśuddhi-kṣaye jñāna-dīptir-āviveka-khyāteḥ

By following aṅgas *or various limbs of Yoga, all* aśuddhi *or impurities are eliminated, giving rise to the light of* Jñāna *or true knowingness and leading to the blossoming of* Viveka *or the faculty enabling one to discern and discriminate (between the rightful course of action and otherwise).*

II.29

yama niyama āsana prāṇāyāma pratyāhāra dhāraṇā dhyāna samādhayo'ṣṭāvaṅgāni

Yama, *self restraint or discipline;* Niyama *or virtuous principles to live by;*

Āsana *or maintaining a comfortable*
posture that is both steady and firm,
as well as comfortable and easy.
(The word āsana *does not refer to a set of*
physical postures alone, as it is commonly
understood, but to a steady
and moderate life style);
Prāṇāyāma *or management of life force*
(by means of regulating one's breath);
Pratyāhāra *or voluntarily withdrawal from*
excesses in any form);
Dhāraṇā *or contemplation;*
Dhyāna *or meditation; and*
Samādhi, *equanimity or enlightenment;*
these are Aṣṭāṅgā *or the Eight Limbs of Yoga*
(to enable one live attentively or meditatively).

II.30

ahiṁsā-satya-asteya
brahmacarya-aparigrahāḥ yamāḥ

Ahiṁsā *or non-injury;*
Satya, *truthfulness, or absentation from falsehood;*
Asteya, *non-stealing, or non-misappropiation;*
Brahmacarya *or avoiding sexual misconduct*
(this implies sexual restraint and use of

conserved energy to become more creative and to gain a strong will power); and Aparigrahā, non-possessiveness or not holding on the non-essentials (this is an injunction against being greedy), these are Yamas, vows for self-restraint or self-discipline.

II.31

jāti-deśa-kāla-samaya-anavacchinnāḥ sārvabhaumā-mahāvratam

These Mahāvrata, great vows or self-disciplinary codes are universal by nature (impliying these are to be adhered to by all practitioners of Yoga) irrespective of their race, country of birth and residence, time, circumstances, and all other worldly or material differences.

II.32

śauca samtoṣa tapaḥ svādhyāy-eśvarapraṇidhānāni niyamāḥ

Śauca, cleanliness or purity;
Samtośa or self-contentment;

Tapaḥ, *self discipline or self-imposed austerities;*
Svādhyāya, *self study or the study of self;*
and Īśvara Praṇidhāna *or submission to the Lord*
who dwells within every being, these are Niyamas,
principles or codes for living virtuously.

II.33

vitarka-bādhane pratiprakṣa-bhāvanam

When disturbing sentiment create bondage,
hold you captive and cause sorrow,
then develop or cultivate the opposite,
the right bhāvanā, *sentimens, or, rather attitude.*

II.34

vitarkā himsādayaḥ
kṛta-kārita-anumoditā
lobha-krodha-moha-āpūrvakā
mṛdu-madhya adhimātrā
duḥkha-ajñāna-ananta-phalā
iti pratiprakṣa-bhāvanam

A single negative sentiment like violence
and the like, accompanied or triggered by such

*negative traits like greed, anger and delusion,
whether acted upon, caused to be acted upon or
even merely approved of
can already cause mild, medium or intense and
endless suffering as well as ignorance
(which, in turn, can create a chain of
ignorant actions, causing more suffering).
Hence, it is advised to develop or cultivate
the opposite (positive) sentiment or attitude.*

II.35

ahiṁsā-pratiṣṭhāyaṁ
tat-sannidhau vairatyāghaḥ

*In the presence of one firmly rooted
in Ahiṁsā or non-violence,
violence can no longer hold its position.
Meaning all violent traits cease.*

II.36

satya-pratiṣṭhāyaṁ
kriyā-phala-āśrayatvam

*The fruit of one's actions, firmly rooted in Satya
or truth, (undoubtedly) correspond with such
truthful actions.*

II.37

asteya-pratiṣṭhāyāṁ
sarvaratn-opasthānam

*Firmly established in Asteya or non-stealing,
one shines like a precious gem
(implying all riches easily come
to such a person.
One becomes truly wealthy, truly rich).*

II.38

brahmacarya pratiṣṭhāyāṁ
vīrya-lābhaḥ

*Firmly established in the practise
of Brahmacarya, sexual restraint or moderation,
one obtains virya, vigor, strength, fearlessness,
or the spirit of heroism.*

II.39

aparigraha-sthairye
janma-kathaṁtā sambodhaḥ

*Steadfast or firm in Aparigraha
or non-possessiveness,
one gains sambodhaḥ, the right understanding*

of "how and what" of existence,
including one's own birth or origin.

II.40

śaucāt svāṅga-jugupsā parairasaṁsargaḥ

From the awareness of Śauca or purity,
rises a sense of disgust (leading to detachment)
toward one's physical body
(implying physical consciousness
that separates us from our true soul-identity)
as well as toward any physical interaction
with others (implying relations
based on physical consciousness).

II.41

sattva-śuddhiḥ saumanasya-ikāgry-endriyajaya-ātmadarśana yogyatvāni ca

From Sattva Śuddhi, true, or rightful purity
arises saumanasya, mindfulness or
a right mental attitude that expresses itself
as eka-agrya, focus, onepointedness,
or singular intention; and indriya jaya, victory or

restraint over senses. Thus, one becomes worthy of
Ātma Darśana *or self-realization.*

II.42

samtoṣāt-anuttamas-sukhalābhaḥ

From Samtosa or contentment,
highest happiness is obtained.

II.43

kāyendriya-siddhir-aśuddhi-kṣayāt tapasaḥ

From Tapaḥ, austerity, or volutarily
self-imposed discipline arises
perfection or excellence in all physical
and sensory undertakings,
thereby destroying all impurities.

II.44

svādhyāyād-iṣṭa-devatā samprayogaḥ

From Svādhyāya, self-study, or the study of "self"
one attains to samprayogah,

union with the Iṣṭa Devatā, or
the Divine Principle one identifies oneself with.

II.45

samādhi siddhiḥ-īśvarapraṇidhānāt

Siddhi, excellence, or perfection in
Samādhi or enlightenment is obtained from Īśvara
Praṇidhāna or submission to the Lord,
the One Indweller within all beings.

II.46

sthira-sukham-āsanam

Āsana is a posture that is both steady,
firm, as well as comfortable and easy.
(Here the word Āsana does not refer
to a set of physical postures alone,
but to a steady and moderate life style.)

II.47

prayatna-śaithilya-ananta-
samāpatti-bhyām

From such (steady and comfortable āsana,
(implying from such life style as explained above)

arises effortless relaxation,
ultimately leading to the union with Ananta,
the endless, the eternal.

II.48

tato dvandvānabhighātaḥ

Thus, there are no more assaults and attacks
caused by the pairs of opposites or duality
(implying one is no longer deluded
by the sense of duality).

II.49

tasmin sati śvāsa-praśvāsyor-gati-vicchedaḥ prāṇāyāmaḥ

Having mastered (the āsana),
one should work on cutting down the gati,
movement or speed of in and out-breath
(slowing down the process
of inhalation and axhalation).
Thus, one can regulate the prāṇa
or life force – this is Prāṇāyāma.

II.50

bāhya-ābhyantara-sthambha vṛttiḥ deśa-kāla-sankhyābhiḥ paridṛṣṭo dīrgha-sūkṣmaḥ

(The process of cutting the speed
or slowing down the breathing is achieved by
means of regulating)
the bāhya, *external or outgoing*
breath (recaka); abhyantara, *internal or incoming*
breath (pūraka); and, stambha,
holding or suppressing the breath (kumbaka)
that must be done with consideration of deśa *or*
place, kāla *or time, and* samkhyā
or number (of rounds).
Thus (by abhyāsa *or consistent practice)*
one can perceive one's breathing
becoming longer and subtler.

II.51

bāhya-ābhyantara viṣaya-akṣepī caturthaḥ

Such regulation of life force or prāṇāyāma
that surpasses or goes beyond the sphere
of inhalation and exhalation of breath

*(as well as the suppressing or holding of it)
is refferred to as the fourth (process).*

II.52

tataḥ kṣīyate prakāśa-āvaraṇam

*Thus, dissolved is the covering obscuring
the Light (the soul consciousness).*

II.53

dhāraṇāsu ca yogyatā manasaḥ

And manaḥ *or mind gains the* yogyatā *or ability to
practice* dhāraṇa *or contemplation.*

II.54

svaviṣaya-asaṁprayoge cittasya
svarūpānukāra-iv-endriyāṇāṁ
pratyāhāraḥ

Thus, Pratyāhāra *or voluntary withdrawal of
the senses from the sense objects becomes easy
as the senses follow the suit of the mind
that has withdrawn itself from the external
(through the practice of* dhāraṇa *or comtemplation)*

*and now rests in its purity as
uncontaminated* citta *or the mind core.*

II.55

tataḥ paramā-vaśyatā indriyāṇām

*Thus arises total, complete, or
utmost command of the senses.*

Vibhuti Pādaḥ

Glory: Do not Stop,
Go Beyond!

III.1

deśa-bandhaḥ cittasya dhāraṇā

Confining the citta *or the mind core
to a limited (mental) area is referred to as* Dhāraṇa
or contemplation.

III.2

tatra pratyayaikatānatā dhyānam

*Ever focusing one's intention or consiousness
(at the mind-core or citta level upon the object
or the purpose of contemplation)
is* Dhyāna *or meditation.*

III.3

tadeva-artha-mātra-nirbhāsaṁ
svarūpa-śūnyam-iva-samādhiḥ

*(Next,) when the object or the purpose
(of* Dhyāna *or meditation)
alone remains, with the* citta
*or mind-core attaining
to the state of* śūnya *or zero-ness
(total emptiness with no modifications*

and no disturbances whatsoever)
that is in reality its original svarūpa *or form, then*
Samādhi, *enlightenment or the state*
of perfect equanimity happens.

III.4

trayam-ekatra saṁyamaḥ

Collectively, these three:
(Dhāraṇa or contemplation,
Dhyāna *or meditation and*
Samādhi *or enlightenment) is called*
Saṁyama *or self-disciplinary*
codes bound together (3-in-1).

III.5

tajjayāt prajñālokaḥ

From the mastery of that (Saṁyama or threesome
of Dhāraṇa *or contemplation,* Dhyāna *or meditation*
and Samādhi *or enlightenment) arises the splendor,*
the light of Prajñā, *true knowingness,*
wisdom, or higher consciousness.

III.6

tasya bhūmiṣu viniyogaḥ

*This (*Prajñā *or wisdom) must be applied
on the ground (meaning in day-to-day living).
This is called* Viniyogaḥ.
*This implies that the practice of certain postures
and breathing exercises alone are not enough. One
must live* Yoga *and diligently
and holistically practice all the limbs).*

III.7

trayam-antarangaṁ pūrvebhyaḥ

*These three (*Saṁyama *or threesome
of* Dhāraṇa *or contemplation,* Dhyāna *or meditation,
and* Samādhi *or enlightenment) are the internal
limbs (related to the mind or the mental/emotional
faculties and intelligence);
hence, distinct from the others
(implying the other five limbs of* Yoga
*are related to the body and physical senses.
However, this does not mean that these three
are more important than the other five
and that one can directly practice these three
by passing all other limbs of* Yoga.

All the limbs of Yoga are equally important,
just like the external organs of human body
are as important as the inner ones.).

III.8

tadapi bahiraṅgaṁ nirbījasya

(However, even) these three –
Dhāraṇa, Dhyāna, *and* Samādhi –
are but outer limbs or features of the state of
Nirbija Samādhi *or seedless enlightenment.*

III.9

vyutthāna-nirodha-saṁskārayoḥ abhibhava-prādurbhāvau nirodhakṣaṇa cittānvayo nirodha-pariṇāmaḥ

When all modifications or fluctuations of
citta *or mind core are instantly*
(automaticaly and effortlessly) restrained
or controlled immediately upon their very
appearance and even the saṁskāra
or impressions of such modifications
or fluctuations do not remain, then (gradually) arise
a new impression of control or restraint.

Thus, the end-result or pariṇāma *is achieved,*
that is a total, complete, and perfect control.

III.10

tasya praśānta-vāhitā saṁskārat

Thus, (by virtue of such new) saṁskāra
or impression of self-restraint,
the very flow or process of self-restraint,
becomes smooth, tranquil and calm.

III.11

sarvārthatā ekāgrātayoḥ
kṣayodayau
cittasya samādhi-pariṇāmaḥ

With the elimination of all distractions
and the rise of ekāgratā *or onepointedness*
of citta *or the mind core, the end-result or* pariṇāma
of Samādhi *or enlightenment*
is attained.

III.12

tataḥ punaḥ śātoditau tulya-pratyayau cittasya-ikāgratā-pariṇāmaḥ

Thus, when the citta *or mind core remains*
Śānta, *calm and undisturbed at all times*
and in the face of all circumstances,
the end result or pariṇāma *of* citta—ekāgratā
or onepointedness of the mind core is achieved.

III.13

etena bhūtendriyeṣu dharma-lakṣaṇa-avasthā pariṇāmā vyākhyātāḥ

By this, as explained (in the previous sutras*),*
stability and harmony of bhūtas *or elements*
(within our physical body as well as outside),
indriya *or senses, dharma or righteousness*
and lakṣaṇa *or one's character*
are attained as the pariṇāma *or end-result.*

III.14

śān-odita-avyapadeśya-
dharmānupātī dharmī

*Dharmī or those who adhere to dharma
or righteousness are ever consistent under all
circumstances, such as* sānta, *calm;* udita, *aroused
(or when the calmness is disturbed
due to certain events or conditions);
as well as in an undetermined,
unknown situation or* avyapadeśya.

III.15

kramānyatvaṁ pariṇāmānyateve
hetuḥ

Different pariṇāmas *or end-results
are caused by following different* krama
or order (of practices).

III.16

pariṇāmatraya-saṁyamāt-
atītānāgata jñānam

As the pariṇāma *or result of the threefold Saṁyama
(*Dhāraṇa, *contemplation;* Dhyāna, *meditation; and*

Samādhi, enlightenment)
one gains knowledge of past,
present and future.

III.17

śabdārtha-pratyayāmām-itaretarādhyāsāt-samkaraḥ tat-pravibhāga-samyamāt sarvabhūta-ruta-jñānam

Confusion arises due to the discord or disharmony between śabda or the spoken words, their artha or meaning and the pratyayāmām or the intention they are spoken with. From Samyama (the trio of Dhāraṇa, contemplation; Dhyāna, meditation; and Samādhi, enlightenment) upon pravibhāga or such distinction one gains knowledge about the true import of words spoken by all living things, all creatures.

III.18

samskāra-sākṣātkaraṇāt pūrva-jāti-jñānam

Knowledge of previous birth is gained by direct observation of the (past) samskāra

*or impressions (which have manifested as one's
character and inherent potentials
as well as natural tendencies).*

III.19

pratyayasya para-citta-jñānam

*By (knowing or direcly perceiving) the content
of one's own* citta *or mind core, one gains
knowledge about the content of another's* citta.

III.20

na ca tat sālambanaṁ tasya-aviṣayī bhūtatvāt

*Such (the knowledge about the content
of* citta *or mind core),
cannot be gained with the support
of external means.*

III.21

kāya-rūpa-saṁyamāt tat-grāhyaśakti-stambhe cakṣuḥ prakāśāsamprayoge'ntardhānam

*With Saṁyama (Dhāraṇa, contemplation;
Dhyāna, meditation; and Samādhi or being
conscious) upon the physical form and suspending
grāhyaśakti or the power of grasping or perception,
one can separate it from cakṣuḥ or
the physical eye and prakāsa or light.
Thus, one becomes invisible (to the
outer world of matter. Meaning, such person
does not bother about the world of
matter, and he is not bothered by it.).*

III.22

Etena śabdādy antardhānam uktam

*Similarly, in the same way
(this refers to the previous sutra),
it is said that the disappearance of sound and
etcetera can be affected.
(Implying one can free himself from the
impact of sounds heard and etcetera).*

III.23

sopa-kramaṁ nirupa-kramaṁ ca karma tatsaṁyamāt-aparāntajñānam ariṣṭebhyo vā

By virtue of Saṁyama *(Dhāraṇa, contemplation;
Dhyāna, meditation; and Samādhi or being
conscious)
upon (the result of)* karmas, *both the ones already
set in motion or active and those which are still
dorment and inactive,
one gains the ability to understand the natural
phenomenon, omens, or signs related to the end of
one's sojourn on earth (implying one gains the fore-
knowledge about one's
physical death).*

III.24

maitry-adiṣu balāni

By virtue of Saṁyama *(Dhāraṇa, contemplation;
Dhyāna, meditation; and Samādhi or being
conscious of)* maitrī, *friendliness, companionship
or togetherness, and so forth,one obtains the
corresponding powers.*

III.25

baleṣu hastibalādīnī

*By virtue of Saṁyama (Dhāraṇa, contemplation;
Dhyāna, meditation; and Samādhi or being
conscious of) bala or (physical) power,
one gains the power of an elephant
and the like.*

III.26

pravṛtty-āloka-nyāsāt sūkṣmā-vyāvahita-viprakṛṣṭa-jñānam

*By casting light (of inner consiousness)
upon the subtle, the concealed and the distant,
one gains knowledge of the same.*

III.27

bhuva-jñānaṁ sūrye-saṁyamāt

*By virtue of Saṁyama (Dhāraṇa or contemplation;
Dhyāna or meditation; and, Samādhi or being
conscious of) the (light of ever effulgent) Sūrya or
the sun, one gains knowledge
about the world.*

III.28

candre tāravyūha-jñānam

By virtue of Saṁyama *(Dhāraṇa or contemplation;*
Dhyāna *or meditation; and* Samādhi *or being
conscious of) the (soothing light of)* Candra
*or the moon, one gains knowledge
about the entire constellation of the stars.*

III.29

dhruve tadgati-jñānam

By virtue of Saṁyama *(Dhāraṇa, contemplation;*
Dhyāna, *meditation; and* Samādhi *or being
conscious of) the polar star, one gains knowledge
of the movement of the stars.*

III.30

nābhicakre kāyavyūha-jñānam

(By virtue of Saṁyama*) on the navel* Cakra
or energy center, knowledge of the vyūha, *the
order, or the working of body is gained.*

III.31

kaṇṭha-kūpe kṣutpipāsā nivṛttiḥ

*(Saṁyama) on the gullet
or the hollow of the throat
ceases hunger and thirst.*

III.32

kūrma-nāḍyāṁ sthairyam

(Saṁyama) on the kūrma nāḍi *(one of the* nāḍis *or
pathways of* prāṇa, *sometime related
with artery and veins, named* kūrma *or tortoise)
brings about stability or firmness.*

III.33

mūrdha-jyotiṣi siddha-darśanam

*(Saṁyama) on the light in the head results in
the* darśana *or vision of the* siddhas,
the perfected beings or accomplished masters.

III.34

prātibhād-vā sarvam

(Saṁyama) *on the* Prātibhā
*or the light of intuition within
enables one to gain the knowledge
of everything (omniscience).*

III.35

hṛdaye citta-saṁvit

(Saṁyama) *on* hṛdaya *or heart
(as the seat of emotions and sensations),
makes one gain the knowledge or
understanding of* citta, *the mind-core.*

III.36

sattva-puruṣāyoḥ atyantā-saṁkīrṇayoḥ pratyayāviśeṣo-bhogaḥ para-arthat-vāt-sva-arthasaṁyamāt puruṣa-jñānam

*One is focused upon bhogaḥ,
or worldly and sensory pleasures*

*and enjoyments because of one's inability
to distinguish Puruṣa or the collective soul,
the true self, from (the qualities of nature or Prakṛti,
including the highest and most noble quality of)
Sattva, calm-dynamism.
(For, all such qualities bind the individual soul
or Jivātma with the material
existence or Prakṛti.)*

III.37

tataḥ prātibha-srāvāṇa-vedana-ādarśa-āsvāda-vārtā jāyante

*Thence (by virtue of various practices
as described in the previous sutras)
is born the ability to hear,
touch, see, taste and smell intuitively*

III.38

te samādhav-upasargā-vyutthāne siddhayaḥ

*(However,) in the state of vyutthāna
when the mind is still focused outward*

(upon the material existence, material comforts
and sensory pleasures)
all (these) siddhis *or accomplishments*
can become obstacles in the attainment of
true Samādhi *or full enlightenment.*

III.39

badnha-kāraṇa-śaithilyāt pracāra-samvedanācca
cittasya paraśarīrāveśaḥ

Having gained freedom from
the cause of bondage
(as explained in the sutras *36 and 37)*
and having gained the true knowingness
or expanded perception of all things,
one can even enter another's body.

III.40

udāna-jayāat jala-paṅkha-kaṇṭakādiṣv-
asaṅgo'tkrāntiśca

By the mastery of udāna *or life force*
that goes up to vitalize the brain,
one can no longer be drowned in the water,

puled by muddy swamp and harmed by a thorn
(anything sharp). Indeed, one can levitate
or rise above them
(one becomes fearless by rising above
physical or material consciousness).

III.41

samāna-jayāj-jvalanam

By the mastery of samāna *or life force*
that vitalizes the middle region of the body,
heat, and even fire, can be produced.

III.42

śrotra-ākāśayoḥ sambandha-
saṁyamāt
divyaṁ śrotram

By virtue of Saṁyama (Dhāraṇa, contemplation;
Dhyāna, meditation; and Samādhi or being
conscious of) the relation between ear and ākāśa
or the etheric substance of the space, one acquires
divine hearing.

III.43

kāyākāśayoḥ sambandha-saṁyamāt laghu-tūla-samāpatteśca-ākāśa gamanam

By virtue of Samyama *(Dhāraṇa, contemplation;* Dhyāna, *meditation; and* Samādhi *or being concious of) the relation between the body and* ākāśa *or the etheric substance of the space and by (mentally) connecting oneself with cotton-wool, one becomes as light as the cotton and gets the ability of easy movement through the space.*

III.44

bahir-akalpitā vṛttiḥ mahā-videhā tataḥ prakāśa-āvaraṇa-kṣayaḥ

(Indeed, by virtue of Samyama - Dhāraṇa, *contemplation;* Dhyāna, *meditation; and* Samādhi, *enlightenment or being concious) one can attain the state of* Mahāvidehā, *that is the state beyond physical as well as mental/emotional and intellectual bodies – hence, referred to as inconceivable or unimaginable.*
Thus, the covering (of delusion)

obstructing the light
(of pure consciousness within)
is destroyed.

III.45

sthūla-svarūpa-sūkṣma-anvaya-arthavattva-saṁyamāt bhūtajayaḥ

By virtue of Saṁyama
*(*Dhāraṇa, *contemplation;* Dhyāna, *meditation;*
and Samādhi *or being conscious of)*
the nature of bhūta *or elements,*
which are gross, constant
as well as subtle and all-pervading,
one gains mastery over all of them.

III.46

tato'ṇimādi-prādurbhāvaḥ
kāyasaṁpat tad-dharānabhighātśca

Thence (having gained mastery over the elements
and transcended them), aṇimā *(the ability to*
decrease the size of one's body and become
smaller than the smallest particle) and all other
siddhis or accomplishments are attained. The body
(physical, vital, mental/emotional and intellectual

layers of consciousness) is so perfected
that the elements can no longer
obstruct its functions.

III.47

rūpa-lāvaṇya-bala-vajra-
saṁhananatvāni kāyasaṁpat

Perfection or excellence of the body consists
of beautiful form, physical strength and vajra or
thunderbolt-like dynamism and firmness.

III.48

grahaṇa-svarūpa-asmitā-avaya-
arthavattva-saṁyamāt-indriya jayaḥ

By virtue of Saṁyama (Dhāraṇa, *contemplation;*
Dhyāna, *meditation; and,* Samādhi *or being*
conscious) upon grahaṇa *or the ability to grasp,*
to know and to understand something,
svarūpa *or one's own form*
(that includes all physical limbs, sense organs
and senses of perception) and asmitā *or the I-ness*
—their individual significance and mutual
connection—
one gains mastery over the senses.

III.49

tato mano-javitvaṁ vikaraṇa-bhāvaḥ pradhāna-jayaś-ca

*Thence (having gained mastery over senses),
manaḥ or mind becomes swift enough
to gain instantaneous victory over* Pradhāna,
Prakṛti, *or material existence,
without the aid of any other tool
(i.e. body, senses, or any other external help).*

III.50

sattva-puruṣa-anyatā-khyātimātrasya sarva-bhāvā-adhiṣṭhātṛtvaṁ sarva-jñātṛtvaṁ ca

*(It is) only then that one gains the ability to discern
and differentiate between* sattva, *the finest quality
of* Pradhāna, Prakṛti *or material existence and*
Puruṣa, *the collective soul-consciousness.*

III.51

tad-vairāgyād-api doṣa-bīja-kṣaye kaivalyam

When one attains to vairāgya, *dispassion,*
or detachment even to that
(to such accomplishments as mentioned
in the previous sutras),
then the seed of all doṣas, *all impediments,*
faults and weaknesses is destroyed.
Thus, giving rise to Kaivalya, *the state of suchness*
or oneness beyond all descriptions.

III.52

sthāny-upa-nimantraṇe saṅga-smaya-akaraṇaṁ punar-aniṣṭa-prasaṅgāt

One should not be attached or become proud
or arrogant on account of being invited
or honored with proximity by people in power
and having authority. For, association with such
may cause harm (this is a reminder that
the supernatural powers gained should not
cause one to become arrogant or proud).

III.53

kṣaṇa-tat-kramayoḥ saṁyamāt vivekajaṁ-jñānam

By virtue of Saṁyama (Dhāraṇa, contemplation; Dhyāna, meditation; and Samādhi or being concious of) this moment and the succeeding moment arises the true knowingness based on viveka, the faculty of discernment.

III.54

jāti-lakṣaṇa-deśaiḥ anyatā-anavacchedāt tulyayoḥ tataḥ pratipattiḥ

Thence (having acquired true knowingness based on viveka or faculty of discernment) one can differentiate even between the similars that are otherwise undistinguishable because of (the similarity of) their origin, quality and place or state. (For instance, the ability to distinguish true humility from the fake make-believe one or true joy and cheerfulness from a fake smile.)

III.55

tārakaṁ sarva-viṣayaṁ sarvathā-viṣayam-akramaṁ-ceti vivekajaṁ jñānam

*The true knowingness born of
and arising from such viveka,
the faculty of discernment,
is truly transcendent and liberates one
from all conditions and objects
(which may create bondage).*

III.56

sattva-puruṣayoḥ śuddhisāmye kaivalyam

*In its purified state, sattva (the finest quality
of the material existence or Prakṛti)
is same as Puruṣa or collective soul, energy.
This, then, is Kaivalya, suchness or oneness.*

Kaivalya Pādaḥ

Suchness/Oneness:
The Ultimate

IV.1

janma-oṣadhi-mantra-tapas-samādhi-jāḥ siddhayaḥ

The siddhis, *various natural
and supernatural powers
and/or excellence in certain fields
are results of birth (in a family and environment
conducive to such accomplishments);*
oṣadhi *or herbs and plants (used as medicine
to correct the various* doṣas *or faults in human
beings, affecting their charactter and mood);* mantra
*or affirmations (to remind oneself of the inner
strength and inherent potentials);*
tapas *or austerities (self-imposed discipline);
or,* samādhi, *enlightenment,
(awareness or living consciously).*

IV.2

jāty-antara-pariṇāmaḥ prakṛty-āpūrāt

Overflow or access of Prakṛti *or existential materials
(arising from obsessions and unfulfilled desires
and taking the shape of inherent potentials and
tendencies) results in rebirth
or taking of other forms.*

IV.3

nimittam-aprayojakaṁ prakṛtīnāṁ-varaṇa-bhedastu tataḥ kṣetrikavat

Like a farmer (irrigating the field,
simply allows the excessive water to flow through;
does nothing else) allows prakṛti
or nature take its own course,
so too a Yogī *allows the inherent tendencies*
and etcetera exhaust themselves
(without further involving the citta *or mind core*
in a new venture that may cause
fresh desires, obsessions, et cetera).

IV.4

nirmāṇa-cittāny-asmitā-mātrāt

Citta *or the mind core is formed*
by asmitā *or i-ness.*

IV.5

pravṛtti-bhede prayojakaṁ cittam-ekam-anekeṣām

Such citta *or mind core*
(formed by or born of asmitā *or i-ness)*
is actually ekaṁprayojaka *or the sole initiator*
of all things and all activities
though it may appear as anekeṣaṁ *or many,*
due to various distinct activities or pravṛtti.

IV.6

tatra dhyānajam-anāśayam

Whereas (all actions born) of
Dhyāna *or meditation*
(activities undertaken meditatively)
are without any residue.
(Meaning neither do they strengthen
citta *or mind-core, nor create*
any new desire and obsession.)

IV.7

karma-aśukla-akṛṣṇaṁ yoginaḥ trividham-itareṣām

*Such (meditative) karmas or actions
of a Yogī are neither white nor black;
whereas, those of others are threefold
(white, black and grey, meaning good,
bad and in between. Hence, they must
bear the consequence of their actions,
whereas a Yogī does not).*

IV.8

tataḥ tad-vipāka-anugṇānām-eva-abhivyaktiḥ vāsanānām

*As a result of such (threefold karmas:
good, bad and in between) arise vāsanā,
unfulfilled desires and obsessions,
manifesting as habits and inclinations.*

IV.9

jāti deśa kāla vyavahitānām-apy-āntaryāṁ
smṛti-saṁskārayoḥ ekarūpatvāt

Saṁskāra or impressions
and smṛti or memories of such saṁskāras
are one and the same.
Together they form a link between
the present and past births
and the place as well as time of birth,
though it may not be apparent.

IV.10

tāsām-anāditvaṁ cāśiṣo nityatvāt

These (vāsanās, desires or obsessions seem to)
have no beginning or anādi, therefore eternal or
nitya. (However, so is) Āśiṣa (or the Grace of God.
Implying that by the Grace of God that
one may also define as the realization of one's
true nature, such obsessions can be overcome).

IV.11

hetu-phala-āśraya-ālambanaiḥ-saṁgṛhītatvāt-eṣām-abhāve-tad-abhāvaḥ

*Since cause and effect are
interconnected, bond or held together,
so the end of the cause
(asmitā or I-ness arising from avīdyā or ignorance
of one's true nature as Soul, and an inseparable
part of the Supreme Soul), brings the effect
(vāsanās or obsessions and
unfulfilled desires leading to rebirth) to an end.*

IV.12

atīta-anāgataṁ svarūpato'sti-adhvabhedād dharmāṇām

*Indeed, both past and future exist
(in the present time) in their respective or actual
forms. The distinction is caused by
dharma or the course of action,
the path choosen (by the mind or manaḥ.
Meaning, as our present experience is
caused by our past actions, similarly
our future experience depends upon
what we do in the present time.)*

IV.13

te vyakta-sūkṣmāḥ guṇa-atmānaḥ

Vyakta, *gross and manifest*
and sūkṣma, *subtle and unmanifest*
(events or happenings in the present time
as well future are all caused by the mind or manaḥ,
some already manifest, others not yet)
follow the natural course of guṇas
(sattva, calm; rajas, dynamic/passionate;
and tamas, static, ignorance, lazyness).

IV.14

pariṇāma-ikatvāt vastu-tattvam

(Having different proportions of the material
qualities of sattva, rajas, *and* tamas) *all vastu or*
material objects are in essence one and the same,
as such their pariṇāma *or end result is also the*
same. (Meaning, they manifest, exist for some time,
and become unmanifest again.)

IV.15

vastusāmye citta-bhedāt-
tayorvibhaktaḥ panthāḥ

*Inspite of the sameness or oneness
of all vastu or natural objects,
(everything in this material existence)
the way* citta *or mindcore
perceives them makes them look different.*

IV.16

na caika-citta-tantraṁ cedvastu
tad-apramāṇakaṁ tadā kiṁ syāt

*Vastu or a material object does not depend upon
the* citta *of a single one being.
There is nothing to prove that. How can it be?
(meaning, if an object can be perfectly defined
based upon the perception of the* citta *of a single
one being and such definition be universal,
acceptable to all, then there should be no conflicts
and no arguments in the world,
which is not the case.)*

IV.17

tad-uparāga-apekṣitvāt cittasya vastu-jñātājñātaṁ

*Knowledge or ignorance about an object is caused
by the expectation or reaction of the* citta,
the mind core, and whether it (the citta)
is drawn to the object or not.

IV.18

sadājñātāḥ citta-vrttayaḥ tat-prabhoḥ puruṣasya-apariṇāmitvāt

*The vṛttis, fluctuations, modifications,
or the changing nature of the* citta, *the mind core is
known due to the changeless
nature of its Master,* Puruṣa,
or the collective soul consciousness.

IV.19

na tat-svābhāsaṁ dṛśyatvāt

Dṛśyatvāt or the object seen and citta,
the mind core perceiving the object

*(both) are not self-illumined.
(Meaning they are not conscious of themselves.
Simply put, they merely work for Puruṣa, the
collective soul that is the consciousness factor.)*

IV.20

eka samaye cobhayāna-avadhāraṇam

*It is not possible to hold on (anavadhāraṇam)
two different things at one and some time
(implying whether one is matter-oriented
or soul-oriented. One cannot be both
at one and the same time.)*

IV.21

cittāntara dṛśye buddhi-buddheḥ atiprasaṅgaḥ smṛti-saṁkaraś-ca

*(Since it is not possible to hold two different things
together as explained in the previous* sutra, *so too)
the* citta *or mind core cannot have a different or
dual-vision and perception (about an object seen),
or stretch itself to access* buddhi, *the intelligence,
without letting go or dropping all the* smṛtis *or*

memories, and saṁkāras *or past impressions.*
(In other words, citta *will have to drop itself*
to become or transform into buddhi *or intelligence.*
Indeed, without smṛti *and* saṁskāra,
citta *cannot exist.)*

IV.22

citer-aprati-saṁkramāyāḥ tad-ākāra-āpattau svabuddhi saṁvedanam

The cognition or knowledge of the happening
or blossoming of buddhi *or intelligence*
is obtained from buddhi *itself (this is referred to as*
svabuddhi *or the perceiving of* buddhi
or intelligence by one's own buddhi *or intelligence*
only), when citta *or mind core is in the state of*
apratisaṁkramāyāḥ, *no longer moving here*
and there or getting entangled with anything
whatsoever. (Meaning the citta *is free of* vṛttis *or*
modifications.)

IV.23

draṣṭṛ-dṛśy-opa-raktaṁ cittaṁ sarva-artham

Citta or the mind core is meaningful
only on account of the impact of
Puruṣa *or collective soul consciousness*
as Draṣṭṛ *or seer; and* Prakṛti *or material existence*
as the Dṛśya *or the object seen.*

IV.24

tad-asaṅkhyeya vāsanābhiḥ citram-api parārtham saṁhatyakāritvāt

Driven by innumerable vāsanās or
unfulfilled desires and obsessions,
or rather, joining them, that (the citta *or mind-core)*
engages itself in various activities for
(what seems to be) another (entity or being).

IV.25

viśeṣa-darśinaḥ ātmabhāva-
bhāvanā-nivṛttiḥ

Having seen the destinction between ātmā *or self*
and the state of becoming (caused by the
citta-vāsanā *co-operation,*
That (the Jivātmā, the individual soul)
withdraws it-"self" from such (state of becoming).

IV.26

tadā viveka-nimnaṁ
kaivalya-prāg-bhāraṁ cittam

Thus, citta *or the mind core that is already*
inclined toward viveka *or the faculty of discretion or*
discernment is moving towards Kaivalya, the state
of Suchness or Oneness.

IV.27

tac-chidreṣu pratyaya-antarāṇi
saṁskārebhyaḥ

Having acquired viveka *or the ability to discern,*
saṁskāras *or past impressions may still give rise to*

*obstacles during the intervening spaces
(when for some reason the* viveka *is at it's low ebb
and* citta *rises its hood again).
One should overcome such obstacles
forcefully and with a strong intention
or will power.*

IV.28

hānam-eṣāṁ kleśavad-uktam

*(The way to) eliminate or remove such obstacles
is the same as in the case of* kleśa *or afflictions as
explained before (by means of* abhyāsa *or intensive
and repetitive practice, in this context,
to consciously withdraw from
situations causing such obstacles).*

IV.29

prasaṁkhyāne'py-akusīdasya sarvathā vivekakhyāteḥ dharma-meghas-samādhiḥ

Whenever viveka, *tha faculty of discretion
and discernment is transcended,
there is nothing to discern or reflect upon*

(meaning there is nothing left to discern,
this refers to a state when buddhi or intelligence is
already firmly established and the ability to discern
becomes an embedded quality of being); and, there
is no longer any interest (in the wordly objects, in
other words, one is no longer drawn towards them)
then one attains to Dharma Megha Sāmadhi,
the state of enlightenment that is referred to
as "clouds of virtues bearing Sāmadhi".

IV.30

tataḥ kleśa-karma-nivṛttiḥ

From that (Dharma Megha or
the shower of Dharma *or virtues)*
there is the elimination or cessation of all karmas,
all actions causing kleśa *or afflictions.*

IV.31

tadā sarva-āvaraṇa-malāpetasya jñānasya-ānantyāt jñeyamalpam

Thus, all the dirt is gone, cleansed,
and the veil covering the infinite knowledge is lifted,
leaving nothing else to be known,
making everything else of little significance.

IV.32

tataḥ kṛtārthānaṁ pariṇāma-krama-samāptir-guṇānām

Thence (with the infinite knowledge acquired
as explained in the previous sutra),
the guṇas *or the qualities of matter in*
constant transmutation with their various
pariṇāmas *or results in succession come to an end*
as their purpose is done.

IV.33

kṣaṇa-pratiyogī pariṇāma-aparānta nirgrāhyaḥ kramaḥ

As aparānta pariṇāma *or the very end result*
(of all that we have been discussing about,
the entire Yogic *practices or* Sādhanā),
even kṣaṇa *or the smallest unit*
of time and its succession
or corelation with another unit is
terminated, transcended.

IV.34

puruṣa-artha-śūnyānāṁ guṇānāṁ-pratiprasavaḥ
kaivalyaṁ svarūpa-pratiṣṭhā vā citiśaktiriti

Thus, devoid af all guṇas *or material qualities,
the* Puruṣa *or soul is majestically reinstated
(*pratiṣṭhā*) to its* Svarūpa *or original form with the*
Citi Śakti *or the Power of Highest Awareness,
Purest Consciousness.
This, then, is that* Kaivalya, *suchness or oneness.
(The* Citi Śakti *is not the same as citta.
The word* Citi *is used for want of a better word.
This is a state of being, when citta or mind core is
fully transcended, and Pure Consciousness alone
remains.)*

YOGA:
THE UNIVERSAL
SINDHU
SPIRITUAL VALUES
FOR ONE AND ALL

≈ a word before we part ≈

*Meditation is not something that a Yogi has to
teach you; you already have the ability
to shut out thoughts.*

Yogācārya **Swami Sivananda (1887-1963)**

*Yoga is an art and science of living…
Yoga is a way to freedom. By its constant
practice, we can free ourselves from fear,
anguish and loneliness.*

Yogācārya **Indra Devi (1899-2002)**

*Yoga is possible for anybody who really wants it.
Yoga is universal.... But don't approach yoga
with a business mind looking for worldly gain.*

Yogācārya K. **Pattabhi Jois (1915-2009)**

*Yoga allows you to rediscover a sense
of wholeness in your life, where you do not feel
like you are constantly trying to fit broken pieces
together.…
Spirituality is not some external goal that one
must seek, but a part of the divine core of each
of us, which we must reveal…*

Do not aim low, you will miss the mark.
Aim high and you will be on a threshold of bliss.

Yogācārya **B.K.S Iyengar (1918-2014)**

The deeper you get into Yoga you realize
it is a spiritual practice.
It's a journey I'm making. I'm heading that way.

Yoga Practitioner **Sting (born 1951)**

Several years ago, a psychiatrist friend of mine drew my attention to the following quotes from renowned psychiatrist and psychotherapist Carl Jung's book psychology and religion, adding, or, rather concluding, "Jung never favored Yoga." Period.

Upon a careful study of what Jung wrote, I observed the contrary. Indeed, Jung is one of those few who foresaw how Yoga would be misunderstood and reduced to a commodity and bonsai-*ed* to suit the market and to meet popular demand. I would like to share with you following passages from his book:

"I know that yoga prides itself on being able to control even the unconscious processes, so that nothing can happen in the psyche as a whole that is not ruled by a supreme consciousness. I have not the slightest doubt that such a condition is more or less possible…. In the East, the inner man has always had such a firm hold on the outer man that the world had no chance of tearing him away from his inner roots; in the West, the outer man gained the ascendancy to such an extent that he was alienated from his innermost being….

"I would not advise anyone to touch yoga without a careful analysis of his unconscious reactions. What is the use of imitating yoga if your dark side remains…..? Yoga in Mayfair or Fifth Avenue, or in any other place which is on the telephone, is a spiritual fake.

"I do not doubt that the Eastern liberation from vices, as well as from virtues,

is coupled with detachment in every respect, so that the yogi is translated beyond this world, and quite inoffensive. But I suspect every European attempt at detachment of being mere liberation from moral considerations. Anybody who tries his hand at yoga ought therefore to be conscious of its far-reaching consequences, or else his so-called quest will remain a futile pastime.

"Yoga practice is unthinkable, and would also be ineffectual, without the ideas on which it is based. It works the physical and the spiritual into one another in an extraordinarily complete way.

"The split in the Western mind therefore makes it impossible at the outset for the intentions of yoga to be realized in any adequate way. It becomes either a strictly religious matter, or else a kind of training like Pelmanism, breath-control, eurhythmies, etc., and not a trace is to be found of the unity and wholeness of nature, which is characteristic of yoga.

"Since Western man can turn everything into a technique, it is true in principle that everything that looks like a method is either dangerous or condemned to futility. In so far as yoga is a form of hygiene, it is as useful to him as any other system. In the deepest sense, however, yoga does not mean this but, if I understand it correctly, a great deal more, namely the final release and detachment of consciousness from all bondage to object and subject.

"But since one cannot detach oneself from something of which one is unconscious, the European must first learn to know his subject. This, in the West, is what one calls the unconscious. Yoga technique applies itself exclusively to the conscious mind and will. Such an *undertaking promises success only when the unconscious has no potential worth mentioning, that is to say, when it does not contain large portions of the personality. If it does, then all conscious effort remains futile, and what comes out of this cramped condition of mind is a caricature or even the exact opposite of the intended result.*

"If I remain so critically averse to yoga, it does not mean that I do not regard this spiritual achievement of the East as one of the greatest things the human mind has ever created. I hope my exposition makes it sufficiently clear that my criticism is directed solely against the application of yoga to the peoples of the West."

Jung has truly understood Yoga and he understands the Western Psyche that is no longer the psyche of the Westerners alone, but also of the so-called "modern" Easterners.

What Jung calls "unconscious" is what Patanjali refers to as *citta*, the mind core or the mind seed. Unless and until this "unconscious" or this *citta* is brought under control and its' modifications and fluctuations are overcome, yoga, or for that matter any similar practice, may only strengthen our conditioned mind.

Indeed, Jung is only repeating the warnings given by Patanjali, as you may have noticed upon a careful study of the *sutra*s.

More than ever, Jung is making sense now in the present times. There are institutions that are not only trying to separate yoga from what they understand and define as philosophy, theology, or misrepresent as Hindu religious doctrine, but also from its very purpose.

Although they cannot damage yoga by such misrepresentation, they have, unfortunately, succeeded in misleading the novice and indeed meddled with their minds, which can be very dangerous and harmful.

Yoga is a holistic philosophy and practice. The Greeks of old, therefore, call the practitioners of yoga *gymnosophist*s, literally meaning "naked men of wisdom". The nakedness, in this case, does not refer to physical nudity, but to the purity of being.

The Ancient Greek Records also tell us about Alexander's meetings with a number of *gymnosophist*s. Two of them, Kalanos or Kalyana Muni and Dandamis or Dandi Muni, may have contributed to his realization of the futility of his mission and prompted him to call it off.

In the words of Paramhansa Yogananda, the renowned author of *Autobiography of a Yogi*:

"Intensely interesting stories have been minutely recorded by Greek historians and others who accompanied or followed after Alexander in his expedition to India…

"The most admirable feature of Alexander's unsuccessful invasion was the deep interest he displayed in Hindu philosophy and in the yogis and holy men whom he encountered from time to time and whose society he eagerly sought. Shortly after the Greek warrior had arrived in Taxila in northern India (in the region around Sindh, now part of the Punjab Province of the Islamic Republic of Pakistan – a.k.) he sent a messenger, Onesikritos, a disciple of the Hellenic school of Diogenes, to fetch an Indian teacher, Dandamis, a great sannyasi of Taxila.

"'Hail to thee, O teacher of Brahmins!' Onesikritos said after seeking out Dandamis in his forest retreat. 'The son of the mighty God Zeus, being Alexander who is the Sovereign Lord of all men, asks you to go to him, and if you comply, he will reward you with great gifts, but if you refuse, he will cut off your head!'

"The yogi received this fairly compulsive invitation calmly, and did not so much as lift up his head from his couch of leaves.

"'I also am a son of Zeus, if Alexander be such,' he commented. 'I want nothing that is Alexander's, for I am content with what I have, while I see that he wanders with his men over sea and land for no advantage, and is never coming to an end of his wanderings.

"'Go and tell Alexander that God the Supreme King is never the Author of insolent wrong, but is the Creator of light, of peace, of life, of water, of the body of man and of souls; He receives all men when death sets them free, being in no way subject to evil disease. He alone is the God of my homage, who abhors slaughter and instigates no wars.

"'Alexander is no god, since he must taste of death,' continued the sage in quiet scorn. 'How can such as he be the world's master, when he has not yet seated himself on a throne of inner universal dominion? Neither as yet has he entered living into Hades, nor does he know the course of the sun through the central regions of the earth, while the nations on its boundaries have not so much as heard his name!'

"After this chastisement, surely the most caustic ever sent to assault the ears of the 'Lord of the World,' the sage added ironically.

"'If Alexander's present dominions be not capacious enough for his desires, let him cross the Ganges River; there he will find a region able to sustain all his men, if the country on this side be too narrow to hold him.

"'Know this, however, that what Alexander offers and the gifts he promises are things to me utterly useless; the things I prize and find of real use and worth are these leaves which are my house, these blooming plants which supply me with daily food, and the water which is my drink; while all *other possessions which are amassed with anxious care are wont to prove ruinous to those who gather them and cause only sorrow and vexation, with which every poor mortal is fully fraught. As for me, I lie upon the forest leaves, and having nothing which requires guarding, close my eyes in tranquil slumber; whereas had I anything to guard, that would banish sleep. The earth supplies me with everything, even as a mother supplies her child with milk. I go wherever I please, and there are no cares with which I am forced to cumber myself.*

"'Should Alexander cut off my head, he cannot also destroy my soul. My head alone, then silent, will remain, leaving the body like a torn garment upon the earth, whence also it was taken. I then, becoming Spirit, shall ascend to my God, who enclosed us all in flesh and left us upon earth to prove whether, when here below, we shall live obedient to His ordinances and who also will require of us all, when

we depart hence to His presence, an account of our life, since He is Judge of all proud wrongdoing; for the groans of the oppressed become the punishment of the oppressor.

"'Let Alexander then terrify with these threats those who wish for wealth and who dread death, for against us these weapons are both alike powerless; the Brahmins neither love gold nor fear death. Go then and tell Alexander this: Dandamis has no need of aught that is yours, and therefore will not go to you, and if you want anything from Dandamis, come you to him.'

"With close attention Alexander received through Onesikritos the message from the yogi, and 'felt a stronger desire than ever to see Dandamis who, though old and naked, was the only antagonist in whom he, the conqueror of many nations, had met more than his match.'

"Alexander succeeded in taking out of India, as his teacher, a true yogi.... Called 'Kalanos' by the Greeks because the saint, a devotee of God in the form of Kali (Mother Goddess – a.k.), greeted everyone by pronouncing Her auspicious name."

Do We Relate with This Yogi Dandamis?

If we do, then we understand what yoga is. Otherwise, we have to reread *Patanjali* and we have to understand what Patanjali says.

It is matter of great concern that most modern practitioners of yoga are not even interested in studying the *sutras*, considering them "not necessary" for their practice. They feel that the yoga postures or *āsanas*—just one of the eight limbs of yoga—can stand on their own without the other limbs and the philosophy upon which the entire system of yoga stands.

"You underestimate the power of the *āsanas*," writes a big name, a name to reckon with upon reading my blogpost on yoga, "they are powerful with or without the other limbs."

Exactly.

And, this exactly is a matter of concern. Indeed, of a great concern. Without intelligence, self-restraint and spiritual as well as human values, proficiency in *āsanas* alone can boost one's ego, endangering not only the practitioner, but also those who come in contact with him or her. Just imagine an insane person in possession of a nuclear technology!

This Little Book is the result of such concern. The advocates of "*āsanas* alone suffice" may argue that "By whatever means and for whatever reason people are drawn to the yoga mat, it is okay. Eventually they get to know what yoga is." Well, a wishful thinking, besides mere knowledge of what yoga actually is does not help either.

Into her mid 70s, Sue (not a real name), who claims to have been practicing and teaching yoga since she was 50, takes pride in showing off her 40 years old boyfriend, "Thanks to yoga, my sexual drive matches his." So, that is Sue's definition of yoga, her purpose of practicing and teaching yoga. And, there are many, many Sues in each and every nook and corner of the planet.

Steve lost his job and took up yoga practice to "combat stress". Within a week, he was "enlightened" and applied for yoga teachers' certification course. Within a month, he was already teaching yoga.

Now, people like Sue and Steve are neither interested in Patanjali, nor in yoga *per se*. Sue wants to hold on to her waning beauty. She wants to reverse the aging process. Whereas, Steve wants to have a new career and make money.

So, business as usual. "Yogi" Steve does not think that smoking is harmful, and Sue is not only busy dating her much younger boyfriend, but also literally feeding him, paying for all his bills. Great! Is that Yoga?

———✤———

Let us move away from Sue**s** and Steve**s**, and turn to Yoga, *Yoga as It is; Yoga as Expounded by Patanjali.* Before we part, I would like to share with you a program entirely based upon yoga, incorporating not only all the limbs of yoga, but also preparing us for Krishna's vision of a *Yogī*—a True Practitioner of Yoga—as mentioned in the *Bhagavad Gita*, another very important treatise on the Yoga practice and philosophy.

Mystic, philosopher and theosophist Annie Besant (1847-1933) summarizes it (Krishna's vision) as follows:

"That the spiritual man need not be a recluse,
that union with the divine Life may be achieved and
maintained in the midst of worldly affairs,
that the obstacles to that union
lie not outside us but within us -
such is the central lesson of the Bhagavad-Gītā."

"The Bhagavad Gita: The Lord's Song"
The Theosophical Publishing House, Adyar, Preface

This Program Called AIM Yoga or Ananda's Integral Meditative Yoga is designed having modern executives with their tight schedule in view. By diligently following the steps presented here, they can already derive full benefit of *Yoga Sādhanā* or pactice.

So, what are we waiting for?

Let us begin our practice, our customized *yoga sādhanā.*

AIM YOGA

ANANDA'S
INTEGRAL MEDITATIVE YOGA

*"Yoga means 'unity'—it means living unified
wholeness in the field of diversity.
My advice is to continue practicing
Yoga on the physical level—
but also to start and continue to practice Yoga
on all other levels—mental, intellectual
and on the level of self-referral,
transcendental consciousness.
On all levels, Yoga will help you to progress
in every way, in every field of life."*

Maharishi Mahesh Yogi (1918 – 2008)
*Founder: Transcendental Meditation
Movement*

The following prerequisites are integral part of our *sādhanā*. These are as important as the Yoga Postures—the various steps of AIM Yoga—we shall be practicing in a while:

1. We All Live in a Natural DC Field, therefore, it is best to do our practice on a *natural bamboo mat* or *100% natural cotton-carpet/beach-towel.* Natural rubber mat is an acceptable substitute, but not the popular synthetic rubber mats, since all synthetic petroleum based products are not compatible with our bio energy or *prāna.*

2. Practice on Empty Stomach, i.e. 4 hours after the last full meal. The ideal time for practice is, therefore, early morning upon waking up, or in the evening before dinner.

3. Yoga is Not a Work-out, but Work-in Spiritual Practice; hence, for a better result, keep your eyes closed during the entire practice.

4. Never Ever Exert Yourself; no force or pressure should ever be used. You must be very comfortable with and about your practice.

5. Maintain the Flow as You Slowly Move from one posture to another. Avoid fast movement.

6. Your Breathing should be Slow and Deep, enabling the smooth flow of bio energy, life force or *prāna*. And, also linked to the postures, i.e. breathe out as you bend; breathe naturally when holding the posture; and, breathe in as you straighten the torso.

7. Diet is an Important Aspect of Yoga Practice, as such switch to healthy vegetarian diet.

8. Drink a Minimum of 1.5-2.0 Liters of Plain Water everyday to flush away all the toxins from the body.

First Posture

Live in the Present Moment

1. Stand relaxed with your feet together and your hands in the *Namaskāra* or *Anjalī Mudrā,* as shown in the illustration. This renowned prayerful *mudrā* or gesture is a reminder of the One Divinity dwelling within all beings and honoring the same.

Inhale slowly and deeply while inflating or expanding your abdomen, and exhale totally and completely while contracting the abdomen. Repeat this 3 to 9 times. At the end of it, affirm thus: **I bow to the Divine within all beings as I commit myself to focusing upon living and working in the present moment.**

Second Posture
Open up to All Possibilities

2. While inhaling deeply and inflating your abdomen, spread both of your arms as shown in the illustration and affirm thus: **I open myself to all possibilities.**

3. While exhaling and contracting your abdomen, bring both of your hands back to the chest with palms together in the *Namaskāra* or *Anjalī Mudrā* again, and affirm: **I accept everything with gratitude.** This can be repeated 3 to 9 times.

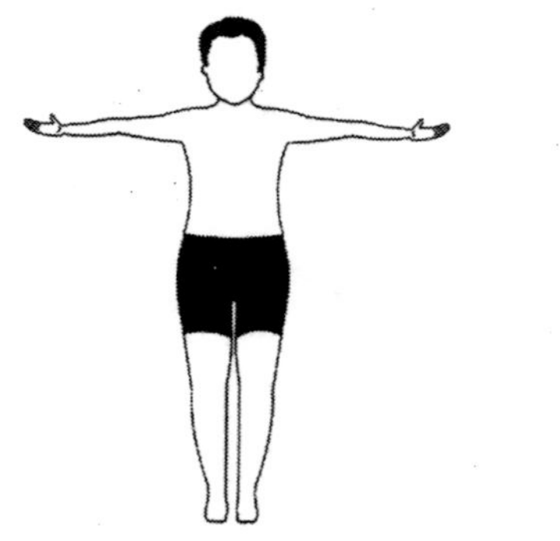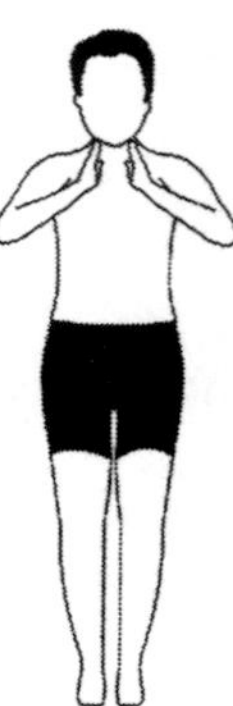

Third Posture

Practice Equanimity

4. Stand relaxed, inhale slowly and deeply while expanding your abdomen, and exhale totally and completely while contracting your abdomen. You can do this few times before moving to the next step.

5. Slide your right arm down/sideward while allowing your body to lilt in unison. Feel your whole body weight upon your right foot and the lightness of the left side of your body. Breathe naturally for sometime before moving to the next step.

6. While inhaling, come back to the standing position. Breathe naturally for sometime and, while exhaling, slide your left arm down/sideward while allowing your body to lilt in unison (the exact opposite of Step 5). Breathe naturally.

7. While inhaling, come back to the standing position. Breathe naturally for sometime and affirm thus: **In pain and pleasure, heat and cold, I keep to my equanimity.**

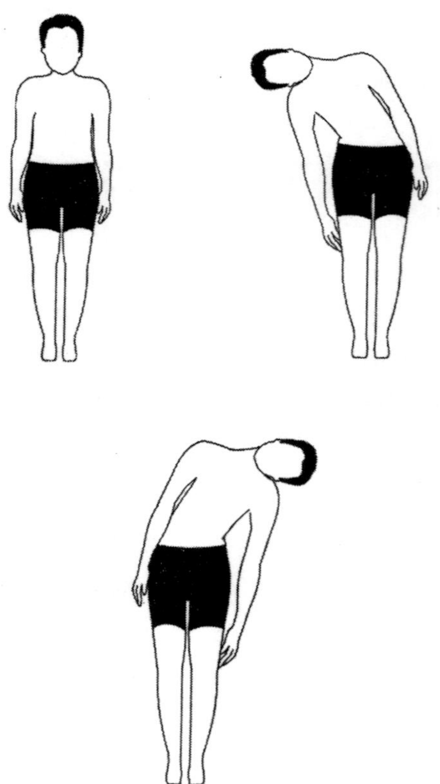

Fourth Posture
Maintain Equilibrium

8. While inhaling slowly and deeply, raise your arms, palms up; at the same time, raising yourself on tiptoe until both of your hands meet above your head.

9. While exhaling totally and completely, lower your arms, turning your palms downward as they reach your shoulder length, at the same time sinking back on your heels. When you have reached the starting position, affirm thus: **High in the skies or down on earth, I remain same.**

Fifth Posture

Overcome Pride and Arrogance

10. While inhaling, raise your head and both arms upward bending your body backward.

11. While exhaling, come to the starting position and slowly bend forward, while raising your arm upward again, as shown in the illustration. You can repeat steps 10 and 11 from 3 to 9 times before moving to the next step.

12. While inhaling, come back to the starting position with your arms hanging by your sides, and affirm thus: **No matter how high I soar, my feet are still grounded on earth.**

Sixth Posture
Cultivate Love

13. Sit erect in a comfortable position.

You may choose *Vajrāsana*, the Thunderbold/ Diamond Posture (on the heels with the calves beneath the thighs, some gap between the knee-caps, and the first toe of both the feet touching each other);

Padmāsana, the Lotus Posture (with the feet placed on the opposing thighs), or any of its variations, i.e. *Ardhapadmāsana*, Half Lotus (placing your right foot on your left thigh, close to your hip – or, the left foot on the right thigh if you find that more comfortable); or

Sukhāsana, simply squat on the ground in cross legged posture. Alternately, those who are not used to sitting on the ground may sit on a chair.

What is most important is that the spine is straight and aligned with the head and neck, ensuring the smooth flow of bio energy, life force or *prāna;* while the shoulders are dropped down and back releasing all the tensions; and, the chest pressed forward, so you are more attentive.

Relax the face, jaw, and belly. Let the tongue rest on the roof of the mouth, just behind the front teeth.

Place your left hand palm upward on your right hand in the way that the tips of your thumbs are touching each other. The hand position is very significant, since the left part of your body is connected with the right hemisphere of your brain governing your intuitive faculty, whereas the right part of your body is connected with the left hemisphere of your brain governing logical thinking.

By placing your left hand upon your right hand, you are affirming the supremacy of your intuitive faculty that is very important for living meditatively. This way you create a circle of energy necessary for cultivating love.

Do the abdominal breathing as usual. Inhale slowly and deeply while inflating or expanding your abdomen; and exhale totally and completely while contracting the abdomen. Repeat this 3 to 9 times.

Now, inhale deeply while raising both of your hands as shown in the illustration, while affirming: **I...**

14. Still inhaling and raising your hands above your head, allow them to meet, lock your fingers as shown, stretch upward and say: **Love the entire existence as...**

15. While exhaling, release your fingers and lower your hands, bring them to your chest crossing eachother, and say: **I love myself.**

Steps 13-15 are inter-related, and so is the affirmation: **I love the entire existence as I love myself.** This must always be remembered so as to maintain the flow of all three steps.

16. Caress your body... Starting with the head, move on until you have caressed all parts of your body, while remembering your affirmation: **I love the entire existence as I love myself.**

Seventh Posture
Motivating Oneself

17. Lie down on your back in *Śavāsana* or Corpse Posture, with both arms and legs spread at about 45 degrees. Do the abdominal breathing until your whole body is completely relaxed.

While enjoying the relaxation, befriend and initiate a mental dialogue with your body. Begin with your legs, advice them to relax, to enjoy the relaxation. As you move upward, talk to each and every part of your body. This may take 3 to 25 minutes, depending upon your need for deeper relaxation as also the time you would like to invest on and for your practice.

18. When you are done, bring your knees to the chest while rolling over to the right in a fetal position, so as not to give any unnecessary shock to your heart. Slowly come back to the sitting position in any of the postures as explained in the Step 13.

19. Do the abdominal breathing for some time, and affirm thus: **Now, I am free of all fears, anxieties, worries, sufferings and etcetera. I am liberated.**

20. Before opening your eyes, thank God, the Almighty, the Existence, or whatever your idea be of the Supreme Force or Energy: **Thank you for this New Day, for this Enlightening Experience.**

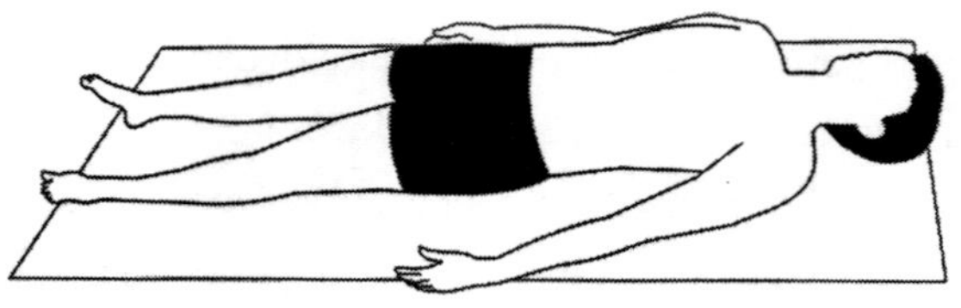

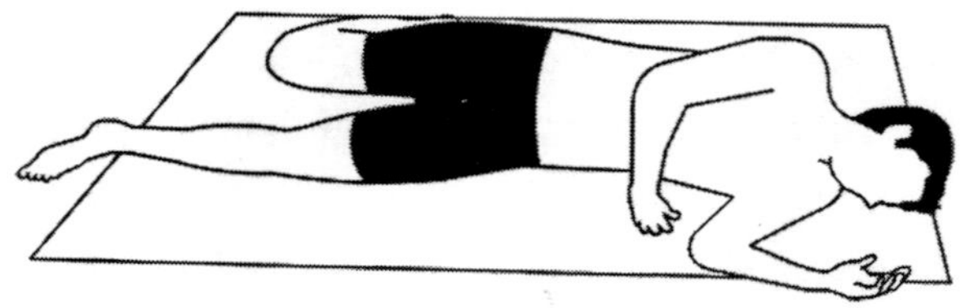

ABOUT THE TRANSCREATOR

Anand Krishna:

No Run-of-the-Mill Spiritual Guru

Reproduced from The Jakarta Post,
August 29, 2006

To sit in the cool tranquil space of the new Anand Krishna center in Bali with the man himself is to be in the company of one of the most renowned spiritual leaders in Indonesia. His talk the night before had been inspirational so The Jakarta Post took the opportunity to meet him to explore further his beliefs about love, religion and peace. His Indian accent was undeniable, yet he was born and raised in Surakarta, Indonesia.

JP: *You said last night in your talk that love is the only solution. Why is it the only solution?*

Anand Krishna: I would say that love is the deepest emotion in human beings. It is the deepest part of our inner selves. When the solution is deep enough, then the result is also quite long-term.

It's just like when you have a tree. If the roots grow deep into the earth, then you will have a big tree. So this is the same thing, we should have a solution that is deep within our being and then we can expect a result which is long term.

JP: *That's a beautiful metaphor. You also said that when we practice consciousness, this is love. Do you have any suggestions as to how we can become more conscious in our lives?*

AK: In Bali, especially, they have a beautiful tradition of dedicating oneself to the environment, to another human being and to God.

I would say that the generic word for God is love. When you do that you are being conscious. You are being conscious of your environment and you are being conscious of anything that you do.

How you sit. How you behave. How you converse with people and interact with them. Consciousness is not something that you can achieve from an hour of meditation every day; it's a full-time job.

It's how you practice meditation in your daily life — from moment to moment. And consciousness also means that it is important to let go of a part of your body in order to save the rest of your body.

JP: *So, to let go of part of your body as you say, is a form of sacrifice. So you do feel that there must be some sacrifices made?*

AK: I think so. We are sacrificing every minute, every moment actually. We are sacrificing certain things, which we feel have lesser value. If you have a better vision, then you let go of the smaller vision of the vision that you no longer have anything to do with now. So actually we are sacrificing every moment.

JP: *It was quite enjoyable to hear your views on Gandhi. You said last night that you didn't agree with his methods of fasting because that was a form of hurting himself and love is not about hurting yourself. What do you think, then, is a better way to achieve peace?*

AK: Bring about awareness. This is why I started admiring Martin Luther King recently. He was so inspired by Gandhi but he didn't use Gandhi's methods. He would go into the street and make his point clear; he would let himself be imprisoned, but he wouldn't fight back or retaliate.

This is the way, I think. You make your point clear and you think about awareness and you make people aware of the cause you are fighting for. This is exactly what I'm trying to do … trying to put these two great people together — Gandhi and Martin Luther King.

This is what is needed in Indonesia to bring about awareness that we are a great nation. Once upon a time we used to export spices to Madagascar and Africa. We used our own ships.

So where is that greatness? That greatness is still there within us. Why do we have to adopt something that is not suitable for us?

What I see in Indonesia is that one part of Indonesia is adapting to the Western way of life, which is quite good; I don't have any problem with this, but the whole culture from the West may not be suitable for this country.

The other part of Indonesia is adapting to the Arabic way of life and this is going to create two societies within one. That's not good because we will bring the fights, the battles and the wars to our side — to our country.

JP: *Your views on religion are very interesting. As you said, we all have many different religions, such as Buddhism, Christianity, Hinduism, Islam, etc, but you feel that we can all come together, because even though we may all have different methods of worshiping God, there is still that one God and one truth that we are all trying to realize.*

How can we overcome our prejudices about religion and become more open and less narrow-minded about the whole concept of what God is?

AK: That's why I like to use the word love, because when you speak of love you talk about love. You can even accept the ideas of those who don't believe in God.

There was a Sufi who met someone who said, "I don't believe in God." The Sufi asked him, "Do you believe in yourself?" The man said, "Yes, I do."

As long as you believe in something — that something can be God, love, or self. In the Indian tradition God is your higher self — so I think we have to create this awareness about love.

There are many people who may think to themselves, "I have nothing to do with God." But all of us have got something to do with love.

So the state of creating a dialog between religions, what has been done especially by Christians and Muslims for the last 2,000 years, has been going on for centuries, yet we are heading nowhere because they are talking about God, yet God is not appearing before us.

When a Christian loves a Muslim or a Buddhist loves a Hindu or a Hindu loves a Muslim and if they are really deeply in love — just two human beings, then they forget about all these barriers.

Instead of talking about God — this is wrong I think — let's talk about love.

Once you talk about love and you develop that feeling of oneness with each other then God is present; then you will have no problems at all.

(Michele Lee, American Journalist
Interviews Anand Krishna for
The Jakarta Post Features)

Anand Krishna as Introduced at the Guru Sangamam Convention

New Delhi, India - April, 12th 2012

Proud of his indian roots, Anand Krishna was born in Indonesia, which as predicted by the **Shuka Nadi** (thousands of years old palm-leaf oracle) is his *Karma Bhoomi* (Workfield).

Dr. Rajendra Prasad, the first President of India remarked upon seeing the child Krishna, "This is not ordinary boy." The prediction has come true. Standing high as the legendary Mount Meru, Anand Krishna wavers not an inch from his course of action, inspite of all kinds of trials and turbulences.

Beside the mother Organization, Anand Ashram Foundation (affiliated with UN), Anand Krishna has inspired several other social and educational institutions.

The 4th President of Indonesia, **KH Abdurrahman Wahid** recognized his contributions and said, "If we want to have peace, then we must hear what Anand Krishna is saying."

He has a legacy of almost 150 books to date (now more than 160) with more than 1 million copies sold in the past 20 years. People of all faiths attending his talks is a running commentary to his vision:

**"ONE EARTH, ONE SKY,
ONE HUMANKIND."**